The Diary of Joseph Jenkinson of Dronfield 1833-43

Edited by Kathleen M. Battye

Derbyshire Record Society
Occasional Paper No. 7
1987

First published 1987

© Editorial Matter Kathleen M. Battye, 1987

The Diary of Joseph Jenkinson is published by kind permission of
Mrs R. K. Judges

Published by the Derbyshire Record Society
9 Caernarvon Close, Chesterfield, S40 3DY

ISBN 0 946324 08 5

Printed by Technical Print Services Ltd, Brentcliffe Avenue, Carlton Road,
Nottingham NG3 7AG

CONTENTS

LIST OF ILLUSTRATIONS

Plate 5 is reproduced by courtesy of Southwark Libraries; the other plates are from line drawings by Frank Ruddock of Dronfield.

PREFACE

THE STIMULUS to write a commentary on Joseph Jenkinson's diary and on the events contained therein, both in his native town of Dronfield in north-east Derbyshire and in London where his life ended, came as much from the fact that studying the diary and its accompanying letters might reveal much about Dronfield at a time when other records are few, as from the fact that, like mountains to be climbed, it was there. Even though Part I lasted only from 16 April to 25 June 1833, this, together with details gleaned from the letters and from references in Part II (1839) and Part III (1843), does contribute information about the period obtainable from no other source.

Joseph Jenkinson's diary first made its public appearance in the 1930s, under the title of 'The Diary of a Radical Hatter', in a radio broadcast by Prof. A.V. Judges, whose wife is a descendant of Joseph Jenkinson's brother-in-law and life-long friend, George Ward. The diary remained in Mrs Judges's possession until she gave it to Mr D.K. Clarebrough, then chairman of the Old Dronfield Society, and allowed it to be transcribed and published. Her cousin, Miss Jennings of Lea Road, Dronfield, then produced a bundle of family papers, including many letters written by Joseph Jenkinson to George Ward after he had left Dronfield to seek his fortune in London. These too were transcribed and studied and it is these, with the diary itself, which form the greater part of the Jenkinson-Ward Collection, shortly to be deposited in the Derbyshire Record Office.

Both diary and letters were transcribed by members of the Dronfield Local History Workshop, whose sessions in Dronfield Library have been held under the auspices of the University of Sheffield Division of Continuing Education. Class members also searched land tax and rate assessments, parish registers, census enumerators' books and newspapers. Without such assistance the writing of this book would have been much more difficult and the class's help is gratefully acknowledged.

Others who have also provided information and access to documents include Dronfield Town Council (Town Clerk Mr Peter Young), Mrs F.C. Layton, Mr Neil Ward, Mr T. Staveley and Mr A. Adlington.

Knowing nothing about hatting when I started reading Joseph Jenkinson's diary, I needed help to explain the processes and terms used and for this I have had the very generous assistance of Dr J.H. Smith of the Extra-Mural Department of Manchester University.

Staff at various libraries have been unfailingly helpful and forbearing, notably in the local studies and reference departments at Chesterfield and Sheffield. In Southwark local studies library I had access not only to map collections and ratebooks but also made use of their knowledge of the area. The help of other libraries is acknowledged in Appendix II and for that too I am grateful.

An account book thought to have belonged to Thomas Jenkinson was a late find, largely as a result of a casual remark on the progress of the work on this book to Mr Malcolm Ford, who had just discovered it in the archives of Dronfield Henry Fanshawe School; to the headmaster, Mr T. Thomas, I am grateful for access to the school to study it.

The manufacture of hats on any scale is not usually associated with Dronfield, whose history is more bound up with edge tools and coalmining, and so the investigation of hatting has added one more dimension to it, as has the evident importance given to national issues at a time when, after a period of relative prosperity, the country was suffering economic decline and a degree of popular disturbance.

January 1987   Kathleen M. Battye

INTRODUCTION

I

JOSEPH JENKINSON was baptised at Dronfield parish church on 22 March 1810, the eldest son and first surviving child of Luke and Elizabeth Jenkinson. Luke was a hatter, as was his brother Thomas, who was two years older. Both men were born in the 1770s and apparently came to Dronfield to live and work after they were married in the early years of the nineteenth century. The census enumeration of 1841 states that Luke and Thomas had been born outside Derbyshire and a pedigree compiled by a descendant gives Sheffield as Thomas's birthplace.[1] Thomas appears to have been the more successful of the two, becoming a freeholder in 1821 and an owner-occupier of land and buildings a few years before that; by virtue of his freeholder's status and land holdings he appears on the electoral register for 1832.[2] Thomas Jenkinson owned and lived in the house on Church Street now known as the Chantry Hotel, which was completely refronted early this century and is structurally part of the adjoining Green Dragon Inn, which he also owned.[3] Luke Jenkinson, on the other hand, by the time his son Joseph began his diary in 1833, was the tenant of a house owned by the Cecils,[4] lords of the manor of Dronfield, the census enumerators' books for 1841 and 1851 implying that it was near the top of Farwater Lane, next to the Manor House. Both men are listed as hatters or hatmakers in local directories between 1828 and 1846 and appear to have had businesses which were distinct from one another, although the precise nature of their operations is never made clear in the diary. When he began his journal in April 1833 Joseph had returned to work for his uncle after a gap of some twelve months, in order to help him at a time when Thomas was without assistance, which suggests that Thomas normally had employees and that the brothers helped one another out from time to time. Joseph could, of course, have been aprenticed to his uncle at an earlier date.

Joseph's references to his work in the diary make it clear that besides complete hats, the Jenkinsons also made hat bodies and blocked and water-proofed them, before despatching them in packs, usually to London, where they would be finished.[5] There seems to have been a substantial business connection between the Dronfield hatters and London before Joseph finally left Dronfield to work in the capital. Unfortunately, there is no firm evidence as to where the hats were made; Thomas Jenkinson owned a building on land below his house, which in the 1851 census was called Bath Cottage and has since been altered to form a small house on Fanshaw Bank today known as Brookside. Features in its structure suggest that it could have been a workshop.[6] In his diary Joseph refers to someone coming to see him 'in the shop' and on another occasion specifically mentions his uncle's shop, but whether he meant a retail shop or workshop or a combination of the two is impossible to say. A rating assessment of c.1846 shows Luke Jenkinson as occupier of a house and shop on

Farwater Lane, with the executors of Thomas his brother, who was dead by this time, as occupiers of unspecified 'premises'.[7]

Apart from the diary there are two main sources for the history of hatmaking in Dronfield, both relating to the years after Joseph had left the town. The first is the census enumeration of 1841, taken at a date when the trade had probably reached its zenith. No fewer than fourteen men gave their occupation as hatter or hatmaker, plus one who was a hatter's apprentice, living with Luke Jenkinson. The Jenkinson households between them accounted for eight of the fifteen, either as members of the family or as hatters living with them, presumably as employees. Of the other seven, one was Thomas Mower, aged 70, who was listed in directories until 1846. Nothing is known of him, nor about the remaining six, who may have been employed by either the Jenkinsons or Mower; one or two may have been in business on their own account.

The other source is a recently discovered account book which probably belonged to Thomas Jenkinson.[8] It covers the years 1834-46 and in its 616 pages contains the names of 1,070 firms and individuals from every part of the British Isles. Sums of money owed to Thomas Jenkinson for hats over the twelve-year period range from small, unrepeated items worth only a few pounds to large regular orders from firms throughout the period worth many hundreds. Business done with one firm in Denton, Manchester, totalled almost £1,748 over five years. There are also accounts for a consignment of hats sent to Jamaica worth £1,233 and another to Canada to the value of £438. It seems extraordinary that a firm doing business on this scale and able to fulfil such orders should have been operating from such a small workshop as the one at Brookside, but no evidence for larger premises exists and it is difficult to trace the development of any of the hatters' firms from their beginnings.

When Thomas and Luke arrived in Dronfield, the name Jenkinson was by no means unknown in the district. The Jenkinsons who lived in the neighbouring parish of Whittington owned land in Dronfield, their tenants being the Lancaster family, associated with Fanshaw Bank Farm across the Lea Brook from Thomas Jenkinson's house. One James Jenkinson died in Dronfield in 1816 and would therefore have been in the town for the early part of the hatter brothers' residence there. Another Jenkinson, Ann, appears in the parish register at the beginning of the nineteenth century, but if any of these were close relatives of Luke and his brother, no previous family link with Dronfield is suggested in Joseph's diary. He does mention various relations without saying where they lived, except when he visited his cousin Ann in Fir Vale, a district of Sheffield; on another occasion he spent the night at an uncle's house in Sheffield. If any of his relatives were hatters, Joseph never mentions that either. The Jenkinsons of Whittington certainly were not. George Jenkinson is described in the parish register as 'gentleman' in 1844 and his son Henry was a manufacturing chemist in Dronfield in 1852.[9]

There is no evidence as to precisely when (or why) Luke and Thomas Jenkinson settled in Dronfield, although it was probably soon after 1800. The population of the township in 1801 was 1,182, with 231 houses in the town itself and the associated hamlets of Stubley, Summerwood, Dronfield Woodhouse, Hill Top and Cowley. Of this population, 100 families were occupied in agriculture and 154 in trade, manufacture or craft. In 1831, when Joseph Jenkinson was 21 and working as a hatter in the town, the population had grown to 1,653. Of the 350 families then, 67 were engaged in agriculture and 211 in trade, manufacture or craft. The growth of population between 1801 and 1831 can be attributed partly to the steadily developing coal, iron and metalworking industries, but when the Jenkinson brothers came to Dronfield the place must still have been predominantly agricultural. Even in 1834, Joseph Jenkinson, who had been in London for more than a year by this time, wrote in nostalgic vein to his brother-in-law George Ward, extolling his native town's rural virtues, where fields were clothed with verdant green, the streams were sweet and clear and the banked lanes spread with flowers. In contrast with London's murky air there was no sign of pollution in this small town scene, at least as recalled by Joseph: 'Not there does smoke becloud the skies, No stench so rank and foul does there arise . . . '.[10]

The place which Joseph remembered with such longing and which attracted not just working craftsmen such as his father and uncle, but also many moderately prosperous families, is described in the *Universal British Directory* for 1792 as 'a small, neat market town pleasantly situated in a valley, surrounded, except on the western side, with verdant eminences crowned with trees, of various hues, and beautifully interlaid with golden plats of shining cornland. The finest springwater in the Kingdom issues abundantly from the rocks, and winds, in serpentine directions, almost through every part'. It was also 'celebrated for an uncommon salubrity of air' and was the home of several respectable families living in its 'numerous pretty buildings'. The salubrious air and the gentility of the inhabitants is a recurring theme in newspaper advertisements of houses for sale in the first two decades of the nineteenth century, while another attraction Dronfield offered its comfortably off residents was a multiplicity of schools and academies for young ladies and young gentlemen, the curriculum of the principal one including mathematics, commerce and navigation as well as the more usual classics, French and drawing.[11]

Joseph does not mention his own education, either in his letters or in the diary, apart from bemoaning his lack of Latin and a wish to improve his grammar.[12]   He may have been a pupil at the free grammar school after it re-opened in 1814 or he may have received instruction in the sabbath school of the Independent Chapel which was begun during the Rev. David Clark's first ministry in Dronfield between 1813 and 1819. The small congregation had been reconstituted in 1812, when a former malthouse beside the Red Lion Inn on the corner of Church Street and Lea Road was demolished and rebuilt as a chapel with a schoolroom beneath. After 1819 the Rev. Thomas Roscoe, who was also a teacher, was minister until 1829, when Clark returned.[13] Wherever Joseph received his education, he was certainly imbued with a zeal for knowledge and believed passionately that education could be the salvation of the poor, lifting them out of the ignorance which kept them from social advancement. All Joseph's references to education are linked to the Sunday schools; he saw them as the proper instrument for the enlightenment of the working class, a view which could well have arisen from his own experience.

Joseph was one of a devoted band of teachers in Clark's chapel Sunday school and it is evident from a letter of August 1833 to the Vicar of Dronfield, William Spencer, that not everyone in the town approved of their activities.[14] It seems that Spencer had invited the teachers to a service in the parish church and had held them up before the congregation as sabbath-breakers, criticising them for teaching subjects other than the 'fear of the Lord'. He did, however, make the mistake of citing King David as an example of didactic excellence, and Joseph was able to point out that David was also a warrior, who combined a great love of music and poetry with politics and enlightened government, accomplishments not at all incompatible with fear of the Lord.

The setting up of new industries and the development of the coal industry in the early nineteenth century meant that Dronfield was leaving its rural past behind and becoming, if not yet a wholly industrial town, then at least one in which there was a growing number of workers engaged in making scythes, sickles and edge tools, as well as working in the foundries and mines.

Among the new enterprises was that owned by the Lucas family, who came to the town a few years after the Jenkinsons. Samuel Lucas, the eldest of three brothers, took out two patents, one in 1792 and the other in 1804, the latter relating to the manufacture of malleable cast iron, the product on which the success of the family's ironworks was based.[15] Edward, Thomas and Samuel came to Sheffield from Birmingham, where their father had been a silver refiner, in the 1780s, Samuel being in partnership eventually with John Read of the Sheffield Smelting Company. He first appeared in Dronfield with his brother Edward in 1811, when he bought a riverside foundry and cutler's works from William Colmore, who with his partner Charles Reeves had developed it from a dyeworks. By 1813 Edward had taken over the business and lived with his numerous family at Vale House, situated on rising ground just above the works.[16] Among other products, Lucas made spindles and flyers for machinery used in the expanding cotton trade.

Luke Jenkinson's family was destined to be closely connected with the other major industrial concern in the Drone valley, that of Ward, Camm and Siddall at the Damstead Works on Mill Lane, which also made spindles and flyers. Luke's daughter, Joseph's younger sister Elizabeth, married George Ward of Damstead

Plate 1: A house on Fanshaw Bank, Dronfield, now known as Brookside, which was probably Thomas Jenkinson's hatting workshop.

House, who was Joseph's best friend and the man to whom he wrote letters shedding light on his own life and character and on events in London and Dronfield between the 1830s and 1850s.

Political and social changes were also in the air as Joseph and his friends grew up. The diary makes it clear that they took great interest in the issues of the day, meeting at the White Swan to read and discuss the London newspapers. Ebenezer Elliott's *Corn-Law Rhymes* and other writings were seized on with relish, although there is no evidence in the diary as to opinion locally on the subject.[17]   Certainly, however, Joseph and his companions were questioning the attitude of the governing classes: there was much criticism of aristocratic ineptitude, echoing the views put forward in the papers they read. These included radical tracts and such publications as the *Derbyshire Patriot* and what Joseph calls the 'Buckingham Review', which were passed from hand to hand at both the White Swan and at meetings of 'the Lodge'.[18]

Much of Joseph's radicalism stemmed from his Sunday visits to Sheffield to listen to the preaching of men like Jabez Bunting, William Dawson and a Mr Berry at the nonconformist chapels in Carver Street, Scotland Street and South Street.[19]   Their sermons offered a scriptural basis for his views and a biblical explanation for the plight of the poor, although he was not content with purely logical argument and pious calls to the deity to help; the preacher was condemned if he showed no fire or heart.

11

In Dronfield itself there was one family whose influence on him was profound, that of Thomas Dobb, first assessed for a chemical works in the land tax of 1818 and listed in Pigot's directory of 1828, along with Robert Ward, as a manufacturer of sugar of lead (lead acetate); he also appears in Glover's directory of 1829 as a manufacturing chemist in partnership with Ward. His son Alexander Forbes Dobb was a friend, perhaps even a mentor, of Joseph's, as is demonstrated by a letter of March 1833,[20] in which he painstakingly answers the younger man's queries on the attitute of God to oppression and slavery, raised by a sermon of Mr Berry's on poverty being a just judgement for sins, an assertion which greatly troubled Joseph. Thomas Dobb was probably the junior partner in the chemical manufactory; Robert Ward lived in Wreakes House on Wreakes Lane, which he may have built, whereas Dobb was tenant of a small house in the town owned by Ward.[21]

Either there was some disagreement between the two (the diary and letters contain several uncomplimentary references to Ward) or trade was insufficient to support them both, for when Joseph's diary opens in April 1833 Thomas Dobb, with his wife and six children, was about to depart for America, leaving a somewhat disconsolate Joseph behind. It is clear that he was expected to emigrate also. The Rev. David Clark lent him *The Emigrant's Guide*,[22] but whatever he may have said to the Dobbs while they made arrangements for a new life, Joseph felt himself bound to his own family. Indeed, the first few pages of his journal reveal his character in a way that the rest of his writings confirm: he was idealistic, zealous, at times passionately vocal, but always drew back from the full implications of his convictions, never really achieving his potential, whether through mute acceptance of filial responsibility, inbuilt caution or lack of resolution. These qualities made him a good son but hindered his career, for he could justify inaction by 'dutiful submission to the dispensations of an over-ruling Providence' and conscientious regard for the wellbeing of his family. A letter to his brother-in-law George Ward makes it plain that both his decision not to emigrate and another unexplained decision some years later involved some personal sacrifice and were taken reluctantly, resulting in a feeling of being unappreciated.[23] He was undoubtedly at the age of twenty-three a very earnest, even pompous, young man whose *amour propre* was easily wounded.

After the Dobbs' departure, Joseph's life resumed its accustomed tenor, a good many diary entries being concerned with visits to the White Swan and with newspapers he read there. He faithfully recorded his own feelings regarding national issues, along with detail from the *Sheffield Iris* or the London papers, usually the *Morning Chronicle,* or at times the *Derbyshire Patriot* and the *Parliamentary Review.* During these months of 1833 there was a good deal of unrest over inequities in the social system and the widespread anger at Parliament's failure to relieve the twin burdens of the Malt Tax and the Window Tax found echoes in the hearts of Joseph and his passionate young friends. Whether they would have gone as far as to join the Birmingham Political Union's call to resist paying taxes or whether they would have lent active support to the *Parliamentary Review's* opinion that change could only be effected by force, can only be a matter for speculation. Joseph's own sympathies are unmistakable and may have been influenced in part by those of David Clark. Both men supported the emancipation of the slaves and on one occasion Clark communicated to his young admirer his disappointment over ministerial measures to compensate slave-owners.

Apart from his interest in politics and religion, Joseph's other preoccupation was with his health; one of the events chronicled at length in the first part of the diary was a bad attack of influenza. There is little else in this part of the diary or later which gives any clue to other aspects of his personal life and throughout his three attempts at journal-keeping he remained coy about his relationship with women. He seemed to be on the point of unburdening himself in the entry for 5 June 1833, when Clark offered to give a feast for the Sunday School teachers and children to which single men might bring companions: 'and here my heart was moved and thoughts across my mind did rush which I won't here transcribe'. But with that the reader has to be content, since the first part of the diary ends with Feast Sunday, 23 June, with no indications as to whether he took a friend to the teachers' feast or not.

Joseph habitually used initials to refer to people; sometimes, as with his employer and colleagues when he went to London, these are men but on other occasions the identity is less obvious. For instance, the 'E.N.' first mentioned on 14 May 1833 could have been Emma North, who wrote to him in October 1854, referring to 'your Miss Miller' in Yorkshire.[24] Miss Miller remains mysterious, unless she stole his heart after the diary ended in 1843, when all appeared to be in disarray and disappointment. There is another unknown in 1843, 'E.C.', who refused invitations, indulged in walks and conversations and in the end told Joseph that he had 'taken a much more enlarged view of the observations than they were intended to furnish'.[25] That she was unquestionably female is confirmed by an advertisement in the *Morning Chronicle* on 19 January 1843, in which E.C. offered her services as a governess to a 'respectable family'. Their meeting place 'M . . . Street' could have been Mount Street, across the river from Southwark, or it could have been Mount Street, off Westminster Bridge Road, where several customers' shops are mentioned in Thomas Jenkinson's account book.[26] The Miss Kennay who acted as intermediary between Joseph and E.C. also appears as 'Miss K.' and has not been further identified. Others are referred to only by ellipses (. . .) and may have been people with whom Joseph had political dealings, possibly the more extreme radicals he met whilst in London in his politically active phase. He also made a number of unexplained visits to Mount Street to spend evenings with anonymous friends; their purpose can only be guessed at.

As to his local social life, he was one of a group of young men who frequently met together at inns or walked together discoursing on the topics of the day. Among these were James Gratton, a tailor and fellow sabbath school teacher; Robert Lee, who appears to have been a woodcutter; John Platts, a spindle-maker who married Joseph's sister Ann; George Seston; George Ward, who became Joseph's brother-in-law and was a manufacturer of spindles and flyers; and Thomas Jenkinson, his contemporary and son of his uncle Thomas, who seems to have taken life a little less seriously than some of his companions. He was found 'rather tipsy with drinking Parson's garnish'[27] in the Red Lion, which used to stand on the corner of Church Street and Lea Road, and appears on another occasion making an obscure joke about 'Dronfield milk'. Thomas also accompanied Joseph and his particular friend George Ward on a stroll one beautiful Sunday morning in the gardens of the Manor House, which according to Joseph was then in a ruinous condition. Joseph waxed almost lyrical about the changes there and likened the desolation he found to that in Goldsmith's 'The Deserted Village'. The church bell interrupted the walk and Joseph was late for Sunday school. He had to pay a penny fine but did it without demur, having, as he said, been one of those who had framed the law on good attendance.

Joseph must have appreciated a brief interval in the fresh air on his day of rest, since on other days he started work at 6 a.m. (on one occasion at 4.30) and finished any time between 7 and 10 p.m. His work included sending off dozens of proofed hats to be finished, rolling stuff hats, making hat bodies, wetting off hats, reckoning the bills and preparing packs of hats for London. At no time does he give the impression that he directed the work of others, nor can it be inferred that he was joined by another craftsman to carry out a particular process, indicating some division of labour. The number of orders in Thomas Jenkinson's account book does, however, suggest that whatever the situation may have been when Joseph was working for his uncle, some division of labour would be necessary as the business grew. Only once, in an ambiguous reference to women being 'remarkably active to get done for the Feast' is there a hint of women being employed, perhaps as tippers in the finishing of hats, although this could have meant merely the cleaning of the house to welcome visitors.

The number of hours worked every day, including Saturday, and the number of hats and bodies made and despatched suggests that business was thriving in 1833; there is certainly no sign of the poor trade mentioned so frequently later in the journal. Joseph must, however, have felt that there was no room in a small town for another master hatter and, being young, he was obviously tempted to make a life elsewhere. He rejected emigration but did have sufficient resolve to go to London, to a firm which was already known to him through business dealings with his father and uncle. Joseph may have left Dronfield soon after writing the letter dated August 1833 to the Rev. William Spencer about the

Old Farwater Lane
Dronfield.

Plate 2: Farwater Lane, Dronfield, from an old postcard. The house on the right was the home of Luke Jenkinson.

Independent Church Sunday school. Even this is not clear, for the last days in Dronfield begin with an entry for 21 June and the rather condescending comment on the women's preparations for the coming feast, the celebration for which centred on the parish church and its patron saint, St John the Baptist. Joseph worked that day until 9 p.m. and does not seem to have looked forward to the holiday with any of the enjoyment felt by his fellow villagers. Indeed, the first part of the diary ends with a somewhat sententious, even sour, account of such observances.

The Jenkinson family, in common with all Dronfield, welcomed friends and relations on Feast Sunday (23 June) whom they had not seen for a year or more. They attended chapel as usual both morning and afternoon, but Joseph wrote that he could not go in the evening, at which he was much grieved, although without saying why. Anglican families would have attended the parish church and made much of their Sunday school children, but others, earning for themselves a few lines of censure from Joseph, celebrated by concluding that they were 'licensed to commit all kinds of excesses to get drunk, fight and to be put under no restraint . . .'. The following day Joseph's life in his native town ended, at least on paper. He came home for two family occasions soon after his departure for London: once for his cousin Thomas's wedding to Sarah Thompson, at which he was a witness, and again in December to perform the same service at the marriage of his sister to George Ward.[28]   Joseph retained

15

great affection for Dronfield and returned from time to time for Christmas or other events; it even seems from a letter to Ward that he seriously considered returning to Dronfield to work,[29]   although nothing came of it and he remained in London to the end of his life.

II

When Joseph resumed his daily writings on 1 September 1839, he made no reference to the six years gap, but left 22 pages blank, as though perhaps intending at some time to fill them with reminiscences of the intervening period. He gives no explanation as to why he stopped so abruptly nor any indication whether some special event or worthy resolution prompted him to start once more. It could be that 1 September was the anniversary of his coming to London. There are some letters between the last diary entry in 1833 and the first in 1839, but they do not help to solve the problem, nor do they establish when Joseph left Dronfield.[30]

Two of these letters, written within days of one another in April 1834, are from Thomas Dobb and his son Forbes in Pennsylvania.[31]   Both make it clear that Joseph had been expected to join them there by October 1833. They looked for him every day, they said, and Mr and Mrs Dobb urged him to bring as many good references as possible with him. Forbes had even obtained a post as a hatter for his friend. But Joseph was deeply offended by the Dobbs' failure to write sooner and the glowing descriptions of life in the New World did not tempt him, even though it seemed that trade was very much more buoyant than in England; the Dobbs were so enthusiastic that they wanted all their Dronfield friends to emigrate, including Edward Lucas.

There are two more letters addressed to Joseph in London. One, dated 9 August 1834, is from his younger brother David, then aged 23, thanking Joseph for his gift of pencils for David and the other teachers at the chapel Sunday school. Joseph apparently still took an interest in its welfare and helped David with his scriptural studies, procuring for him items such as a map of Palestine, which David could not obtain in Dronfield and which was sent via the Rev. David Clark, who had seen Joseph in London. It seems too from this letter that Joseph encouraged his younger brother's efforts at self-education, although he was not always accorded the respect he may have felt he deserved, for David rather pertly pointed out some of Joseph's own grammatical errors to him. He also said that since he was busy at work he did not have much time to read the book which Joseph recommended: Isaac Watts's *On the Human Mind*. David seems to have been a more cheerful character than his elder brother. He stressed his satisfaction at Joseph's gift of a flute as against the offer to send him some

16

old books but hastened to reassure his brother that he would often 'have the pleasure of leading a tune to some delightful hymn with our happy band when seated round the fire on a winter's evening'.

The other letter dated December 1834 is the one with the poem mentioned on page 9, from Joseph to his brother-in-law George Ward. It reveals a fair degree of homesickness, perhaps because Christmas was approaching and Joseph still did not know whether he would be home. He longed for the Dronfield countryside and it really did seem that he was contemplating leaving, for he ended:

> This is a place of misery at best.
> To which ere long I hope to bid Adieu
> And come to live a rural life with you.

But this was not to be and Joseph was still complaining about London's dark fogs when he began the second part of his diary nearly five years later.

This section covers almost seven weeks and is much concerned with the poor state of trade. The economic situation in Great Britain was steadily worsening throughout 1838-9, the result of a financial crisis in America, and it is obvious from Joseph's frequently expressed anxiety over the scarcity of orders that, in the hatting trade at least, things were far from satisfactory. The day-to-day routine of hat making is also mentioned very often, where it concerned the sending off and receiving of orders and the materials and methods used. The names of hat-making firms and suppliers are given, together with details of journeys undertaken by representatives of the firm Joseph worked for in search of orders. The owner of the firm was a T. Irwin and Joseph, who in one diary entry said that he came to London 'at Mr Irwin's urgent request', was his foreman[32] assisted by John Irwin, possibly a son, who was under Joseph and perhaps still in his apprenticeship; also on the staff were a Mr Scott and a Mr Rittson, who were the travellers; an unspecified number of dyers, finishers and tippers; and a certain Mr Slyfield, with whom Joseph did not get on at all well and to whom he referred sometimes as 'Mr Wouldbe' and at others scathingly as a puppy scarcely out of his teens; he was probably in charge of the counting-house or the office.

Joseph never reveals in the diary the actual location of the premises where he worked and near which he probably lived, but in Robson's London directory of 1839 T. Irwin & Co. are given as hat manufacturers of Bridge Street, Southwark. Pigot's directory of the same year gives the further detail of Morris Place, Southwark Bridge Road; Morris Place was the Morris Court shown on Harwood's plan of London of 1819 as a short cul-de-sac off Bridge Street very near the bridge itself. In a letter of 30 October 1840,[33] in which he mentioned a fire in the model room of an engineer called Samuda, which spread to Rosling's neighbouring timber yard, Joseph described Irwin's stuff stores as being adjacent to Rosling's saw-mill 'under the dry arches of the bridge'. Morris Place or Court was widened and extended in 1839 to form Sumner Street, where Samuda's premises were in 1842.[34]   It is possible that Irwins moved from Morris Court to other premises nearer Southwark Bridge or that the stuff stores were separate from the main works and located under the arches.

Irwins had customers and suppliers over a wide area of the British Isles; [35] they also had dealings with Lumsden & Co. of Tralee and mention is made of 'a good business letter from Mr Rittson from Dublin'. The two travellers had regular routes, referred to by Joseph as the Midland journey and the Western journey; Scott also went by steamer to Hull on his Northern journey in the period covered by Part III of the diary. Packs of hats were sent to and received regularly from Rugeley and Dronfield: sometimes finished hats, sometimes hat bodies, reminiscent of the process in Dronfield noted in Part I of the diary. Firms mentioned include both those who were themselves manufacturers, such as Fullers of Long Lane, Southwark, and some who were drapers, tailors and clothiers selling hats, such as Leech & Robinson of Oxford, Tate of Liverpool, Harrisons of Denton, Coopers of Ashton and Scotts of Wakefield. Suppliers of nutria sides, beaver, cheek beaver, red wool, bodies and materials such as pods of verdigris included Borrodailes (principally), Coopers, Paynes, Higgits, Bates and Fullers.

Irwin himself, anticipating the poor outlook for trade, told Joseph on 20 September 1839 not to stock many ruffed hats, 'either gray, black or finished, but say 100 or 150 dozen bodies won't harm, because we have all the materials in stock'. This is one of the occasions in the diary when details of the firm's stock are mentioned. The only other definite reference to stock occurs on 17 October, when finished hats amounted to 45 dozen of all sorts.

The hats made by Irwins were mainly fur - beaver, nutria and so on - but changing fashion was making silk hats popular[36]   and although it is clear that Joseph, in common with most felt hatmakers, regarded silk hatmaking as inferior to his own craft, being less skilled, his decision on 24 October 1839 to learn how to make silk hats shows him preparing himself for something he saw as a future necessity and he was evidently gratified by the success of his work. The silk finishers he referred to seemed to be in Irwin's employ and so the firm may already have been making silk hats.

Since coming to London, Joseph could not have been so regular in his Sunday attendance at chapel as formerly, for only once did he mention going to the 'chapel at the bottom of Union Street';[37] he gave the text but did not indulge in the detailed exposition of the sermon customary in Part I. His Sundays were spent in what would previously have been condemned as frivolous pursuits such as going by steamer to Chelsea or Greenwich, sightseeing with friends or taking walks, all of which activities were accompanied by stops at various public houses. Joseph's evenings were largely spent in similar pursuits, but he did make some effort to regulate 'the foolish way' in which he and John Irwin, who accompanied him on many of these expeditions, spent their leisure and some of their money. He characteristically resolved to make amends by reading Watts's *Logic* through in sixteen days and reading it a second time to make notes. It was after this that Joseph went to the Union Street chapel.

Before mending his ways, Joseph described an evening visit to Surrey Zoological Gardens at Walworth to see a firework display imitating the eruption of Mount Hecla and another to Astley's Royal Amphitheatre, a very popular place of entertainment of the period, featuring brilliant equestrian turns, where he was much interested in and surprised by the various feats performed, leading him to ponder at length on the 'remarkable powers and ingenuity of man especially when directed to any particular object'.[38] Joseph also described a visit to 'a low public house', solely, as he explained, for the purpose of observing a company collected there to raffle off two birds for the benefit of one of the dyers, now unemployed. The men and women were chiefly Irish and did not impress Joseph favourably. He launched into a lengthy defence of education, saying that all the destitution, dancing and bawling, the wasting of time so frivolously and the spending of money so lavishly showed that these people did not value the education which Joseph thought might have helped them to a prospective view of their future wants and alleviated their wretchedness.

Another occasion which prompted him to much pondering and thought was his visit to Gravesend to bid farewell to Edward Hoyle from Oldham and his

WHITE SWAN CHESTERFIELD RD. DRONFIELD '75

Plate 3: The White Swan, Dronfield. The portion to the right is the oldest part of the building.

19

fourteen year old sister, who were embarking for America on the *British Queen*.[39]   Joseph went on board the vessel and saw many sights which moved him to quasi-poetic outpourings on the pangs of leaving home and kindred for the unknown. He was, however, sufficiently down-to-earth to record that he 'partook of some biscuit and cheese and a bottle of Dublin stout', being then able to say that not only had he seen the latest marvel of the age, but that he had eaten and drunk aboard her as well.

Joseph's political life is not mentioned much in 1839, but two incidents and several references to newspaper accounts of contemporary events reaffirm his Radical leanings and his sympathy with unjustly treated working men, particularly, of course, those who were industrious. A day of reflecting on the poor state of trade and the lack of work in his own line prompted an impassioned outburst against a government policy which had brought so many 'industrious and enterprising merchants and tradesmen to be inevitably ruined' and 'laborious and skillful mechanics and artisans . . . into the most grievous distress'. A visit to the West India Dock to pick some logwood and the sight of so many ships with cargoes of sugar, rum and woods of various kinds stored in huge copper-roofed warehouses produced a vehement outcry against 'the lazy band of Aristocratic Legislators who have neither the skill nor the enterprise to engage in such vast undertakings'. All Joseph's rage against ineptitude and injustice was poured out; he showed the free trader's scorn for policies which did not allow the exchange of home-produced goods for surplus food from abroad at a time of hardship amongst the artisan class and he inveighed bitterly that workmen were unemployed 'all to serve the purpose of the Land-owning Lawmakers'.

This journal entry ends with Joseph's assertion, not to be realised, that the poor state of trade, the bad harvest and the fact that there was only two or three million in the Bank of England would all make it impossible to prevent a change in the Corn Laws in the next session of Parliament. He was no doubt thinking that the Anti-Corn-Law League, which had been formed in March 1839 with the single-minded intention of total repeal, would very soon be successful. Holding the political views that he did, and having shown considerable interest in the anti-Corn-Law writings of Ebenezer Elliott while still in Dronfield, Joseph must have watched with great excitement the arrival in London in February of delegates from various anti-Corn-Law associations to take part in a conference designed to persuade Parliament to hear their case before the bar of the House. He must have been equally disappointed when the plan failed. The Anti-Corn-Law League was formed as a result to carry on the agitation in the country at large. There are no direct references in the diary to any discussion he might have had with others about Corn Law repeal, but his preoccupation with the bad state of trade and the reason for it must surely have led him to be outspoken other than in the diary. He did not mention Chartism until 1843, but the Chartists were also active in 1839 and their six-point charter would have appealed to his sense of justice. He referred on 29 September 1839 to a meeting in Deverall Street (off the Old Kent Road), after which he came home 'not very well pleased with what had transpired there', but that is the only entry which might suggest any possible political activity.

Three letters to George Ward, dating from the period between the second and third parts of the diary, shed a little more light on Joseph's life in London.[40] The first, dated 16 February 1840, mentioned the panic then prevailing over conditions of trade generally, but suggests that George Ward's spindle manufacturing concern at Dronfield's Damstead Works was comparatively well off for business. The letter continues with a detailed description of the celebrations in London on the marriage of Queen Victoria and Prince Albert, Joseph not forgetting to state firmly that he was no worshipper of royalty abstractedly considered and mentioning 'that base m.rd. . .r the King of Hanover and the bloodthirsty crew by whom his views and pretensions are supported'.[41] Notwithstanding these protestations, Joseph and his nineteen year old brother James, who was now with him in London learning the hatting craft, seem to have enjoyed themselves mightily. This long letter also refers to an election in January 1840.[42] Joseph had been given a ticket by Irwin, costing 15s, to go to a public dinner in honour of H. Wood, the newly elected M.P. for the Borough of Southwark, at which Charles Tennyson d'Eyncourt, Daniel O'Connell, Joseph Hume, and a Mr Byng were among the 350 guests.[43] Joseph much admired O'Connell and his talent for 'speaking so precisely to suit the occasion and the company', the subject that evening being the Tory doctrine on the pacification of Ireland.

The second, very lengthy letter, dated 30 October 1840 begins by reproaching Ward for not writing and goes on to enquire whether what Joseph called 'the rating or more properly the ratten party' had proceeded further against George. The use of the word 'ratten'[44] suggests that Ward thought that his share of the rating valuation of Dronfield, finally completed about 1846, was so high as to ruin him; rattening parties were giving much trouble at that time in the area with their machinery wrecking activities. Joseph also asked what was being done under the enclosure Act, since Dronfield's remaining hundred or so acres of common grazing and waste were enclosed that year. But the main body of the letter contains Joseph's vivid account of the fire at Samuda's neighbouring business premises (see page 17); the burning embers from their blazing model room and a large wooden building thickly covered the road outside Irwins. The conflagration spread in spite of the efforts of ten or twelve engines, and Rosling's timber yard caught fire too. The powerful floating engine moored by the bridge, which could throw 80 tons of water a minute, was brought into play, but even so, £3,000 worth of damage was caused and Irwin's stuff store adjacent to Rosling's saw-mills was threatened.

The story of the fire also revealed a lighter, personal aspect of Joseph's

21

London life. It seems that he still sent his washing home, for his brother David remarked with some concern on the condition of one of Joseph's stockings, damaged as he hurriedly dressed on the raising of the alarm. There are several diary references to packs of linen going back and forth to Dronfield.

The third letter, dated 21 September 1841, suggests that Joseph was becoming actively involved in the agitation for the repeal of the Corn Laws. It gives an account of a meeting in the Town Hall, Southwark Borough High Street, on 20 September, which called on the Queen not to prorogue Parliament until the Corn Laws had been considered, during which there were a number of able speeches, including one from 'your humble servant' (i.e. Joseph) which was of sufficient merit to be mentioned in *The Times* the following day and commended by I.Q. Harris, MP.[45]   *The Times* also rather scathingly referred to 'apron'd gentlemen who earn an honest livelihood in the hat manufactories' and so it seems that Joseph was not the only politically aware hatter in Southwark.

III

Joseph restarted his diary on 1 January 1843 with a New Year resolution, which shared the same fate as many another, for this fresh attempt ended a bare six weeks later. This was in spite of his avowed determination not to allow foibles - which he did not explain - to divert him and his belief that his 'more intimate acquaintance with business' would prevent him being annoyed and frustrate his intention. Short though they were, these six weeks were important in Joseph's life, for in them the strands of his career in London became once more intertwined and then broken, in one case by his own decision, in a second by Irwin's illness and poor business prospects and in the third perhaps by unkind fate, his own ineptitude or what might be seen as feminine caprice.

It is clear that the fifteen-month gap between the letter to George Ward in September 1841 and the new diary had done nothing to diminish Joseph's radical leanings. His support for the Anti-Corn-Law League must have continued unabated during this time, although whether he was ever a member or made any financial contribution is not known. Living in London in 1843 when the League established its headquarters there and began to organise local collections, he would certainly be caught up in the excitement of the campaign; his speech of September 1841 may even have brought him to the attention of the organisers. It is difficult to be sure how actively Joseph was involved. His philosophical commitment was never in doubt, for it was frequently and forcibly expressed. He also recorded his attendance at a Chartist meeting on 11 January and at a lecture on the Corn Laws by one Timothy Falvey[46] the following day. It could be that there was some indecision in his mind as to which cause should have his allegiance. Joseph was certainly in favour of Chartist aims, as earlier diary entries demonstrate, but after the second petition was rejected in May 1842 Chartism lost some of its impetus and was beset both by sectional differences and the growing power of the League. In spite of hoping that the Leaguers would see the sense in 'restoring the House of Commons to its rightful owners the people' (2 February), Joseph must have thought the dream of universal manhood suffrage was slipping away. In 1843 the League was stepping up its campaign to alter the balance of the parties in the Commons, which Joseph supported, but he knew that his other political ideal of universal suffrage would not be won through the League's efforts. His attendance at both League and Chartist lectures perhaps indicates a genuine search for the best course, but it was a Chartist meeting in Southwark which finally ended his active involvement in all reform agitation.

On 7 February Joseph went to what he described as a tea party and ball at Baxter's, Union Street,[47] organised to raise money for the delegation to the Birmingham Chartist conference the following September. He himself was vice-chairman, with Feargus O'Connor in the chair;[48] also present were Jonathan Bairstow, full-time organiser of the Leicester and Nottinghamshire branch of the Chartist Association of Midland Counties, and John Cleave, one of the leaders of the London Working Men's Association, both of whom addressed the meeting. According to Joseph, all went well, but something transpired there to end his active commitment to any political cause. His mode of expression

High Street Dronfield

Plate 4: High Street, Dronfield, showing the Peel Monument.

suggests that his decision stemmed as much from his old complaint of wounded pride as much as an ostensible desire to devote more time to business. He also betrayed a certain apprehension at being part of what in 1843 often looked like a violent party whose members could fall foul of the law. Whether Joseph returned to his support for the League when it became obvious that Peel meant to repeal must be in doubt, although there is no direct evidence either way. The same applies to his Chartist sympathies, in spite of his protestations of 8 February.

Joseph may have been included in the group who in 1854 contributed to a monument in Dronfield to Sir Robert Peel, who died in 1850, commemorating Corn Law Repeal in 1846.[49] His name does not appear in the newspaper report of its inauguration, although those of his cousin Thomas and fellow sabbath school teacher James Gratton do.

It seems that Joseph's experience in 1843, political, commercial and personal, extinguished the last of his youthful fire, for his later letters speak only of business and domestic matters, making him sound sedate and middle-aged for one still in his early thirties.

The diary entries of 1843 show a business world hardly less disturbed than that of 1839, with few orders coming back from the travellers. On 18 January he recorded that Irwin had returned from a journey looking ill and a few days later, in spite of the fact that during the same week better wages had been paid to employees than for many weeks previously, Joseph was much grieved, saying that Irwin must either increase business or reduce expenditure. His situation seems to have been common knowledge, since a trade acquaintance, George Booth of Denton, offered Joseph a position should he ever be in want of one. Probably feeling the need of some wise advice, Joseph discussed matters with his friend Embleton,[50] eliciting from him a promise to talk with Irwin on the state of affairs. A few days later, Joseph recorded that Irwin had not been at business all day and feared for the consequences, rightly as it turned out. The following day Mrs Irwin came to say her husband was seriously ill with a 'kind of fever arising from colds and also an affection of the liver', although the last diary entry reported that 'Governor' was better. Whether he or the business recovered is unlikely, however, since by October 1844 Joseph was writing on paper headed 'John Fuller & Co, Hat Manufacturers, 95 & 96 Long Lane, Southwark', for whom by that time he appeared to work, perhaps as a traveller, since he mentioned his many journeys.[51] There is one reference in this letter to Irwin and to Scott, last mentioned in January 1843 setting off for Hull on board the *Water Witch* in search of orders.[52] Scott, Joseph told his father, was dead of a nervous affliction, having broken down completely 'under the effects of our disastrous affair at the bridge'.[53] Whatever this may have been, Joseph continued to live in Southwark. The rate books for St Saviour's parish show him as occupier of a house and premises at 82 Redcross Street, not far from the former Morris Court and parallel to Southwark Bridge Road, from March 1845 to October 1848; it also seems from three references in Thomas Jenkinson's account book that he was conducting some business from this address.

Joseph's personal life in this period is as much of a mystery as ever, many of the diary entries containing tantalisingly coy ellipses and unattributable initials, particularly to the E.C. already referred to above (page 13). He never married, although he did not shun feminine society. On the other hand, his letters to Ward reveal a deep affection for his brother-in-law and boyhood friend. In October 1840, when Ward had not written for some time, Joseph pleaded with him to send news and reminded him of their past sympathy for one another, saying 'I could almost write as if my address were to a female of whom I was enamoured'.[54] The fragmentary and prim nature of Joseph's diary keeping does not shed much light on this aspect of his nature and the letters after 1843 reveal only an avuncular interest in Ward's growing family and a kindly concern for his own younger brothers and sisters.

As to the situation of the Dronfield hatters, they were presumably just as badly affected by adverse trade as those elsewhere. Thomas Jenkinson's account book suggests that he could have been better cushioned against bad times than his brother Luke; certainly his will shows his Dronfield property intact.[55] Luke, however, seemed to be in difficulties. Joseph's letter from Fullers in 1844 urged hard work as the solution and implied that his younger brothers David, James and John were working with their father. He offered to pay those who were troubling his father for money and sent sufficient to pay for flour and potatoes and to buy a pig or a side of pork, so that his parents could 'face the winter a little'. In September 1848, in a letter to George Ward, Joseph said that he had sent some wool and a few blocks for children's rustics, which were ordered and, he hoped, would keep his father going until Christmas, when he intended to come home with James, who was evidently with him in London, bringing also an apprentice to keep an eye on things.[56] In the event, Luke died two months later.

Joseph's brother David had been in business as a hatter in Sheffield High Street in 1841 but, perhaps in response to his father's difficulties, had returned to Dronfield and was occupying premises as a hatter there in 1846 and in 1851, when he had an apprentice from Lambeth.[57] David, however, had diversified, for he was also a shoemaker, leaving hatmaking altogether by 1857, after which he is variously described as a book-keeper, commission agent and colliery manager.[58] He died in 1885 at his son's home at Dropping Well near Rotherham.

Joseph's other brothers became involved in hatting for a time, James and Thomas having joined him in London in 1848 after their father's death. It seems, however, that there were no Jenkinsons of either Thomas or Luke's families practising the craft after 1860, although female relatives later in the nineteenth century and into living memory kept shops in the town which sold hats among other things, one on High Street and another on Sheffield Road, opposite the bottom of Soaper Lane.

As for Joseph himself, it appears that he left Fullers some time between October 1844 and September 1848, for then and in May 1849 and December 1851 he wrote from 10 Cheapside, where Edward Felix was a hat manufacturer in 1852.[59]   The *Post Office Directory* of 1856, the year of Joseph's death, lists Joseph Jenkinson & Co at 22 Cannon Street, Westminster, so he had evidently set up in business on his own account since 1851.

Whatever his position in the shrinking world of beaver hatmaking Joseph retained an abiding affection for Dronfield. In his letter to Ward of 1848 he told his friend that all he really wanted was to be with those he loved - to be, as he put it, 'at home, homely', as much for his own happiness as to help the other members of his family, among whom was his widowed mother. His last surviving letter, of December 1851, is mainly concerned with warning of the arrival of a tea-chest containing Christmas presents which he had despatched by carrier from London. There were bloaters to be shared between the Wards and Mrs Jenkinson, who also had some oranges for her grandchildren and a pack of groceries for herself. Ward received a timepiece, the twin of Joseph's own, which is still in the possession of one of his descendants.[60]

No more is heard of Joseph, apart from the letter dated October 1854 from Emma North referred to above (page 13), an echo of the distant past before his departure for London in 1833.

The last two letters in the Jenkinson-Ward collection are from a Mr Rablah to George Ward, the first dated 'Circulation Department, GPO, 4 March 1856', in which Rablah informed Ward that Joseph was ill with a combined attack of rheumatic gout and dysentery and that he was in considerable danger, Dr Lobb having expressed doubt as to the final result. The second letter, dated 6 March, is from Mrs Rablah, 25 Princes Square, Kennington. Her husband had been with Joseph all night and he was little or no better. She left it to Ward as to whether he would come but said that the doctors thought the disease might terminate fatally in less than 24 hours. Joseph in fact died on 10 March at the age of 46 and was buried in Dronfield churchyard on the 16th. His body, in an elm coffin with a case of English oak, was transported by rail as far as Chesterfield, the arrangements having been made by a Cripplegate carpenter and undertaker named Gardner, at a total cost, including making the coffin and case, seeing to the inscriptions and carrying it to the railway, of £19 4s.[61]

Plate 5:   Borough High Street, Southwark, in 1837.

NOTES TO INTRODUCTION

1. Derbyshire Record Office (DRO), Jenkinson-Ward Collection; information from Mrs Judges. The Jenkinson-Ward Collection, which includes the Diary of Joseph Jenkinson and a quantity of correspondence, is referred to hereafter as JWC. It will be deposited in the DRO shortly after the appearance of this publication.

2. DRO, Quarter Sessions: Freeholders' List, Dronfield, 1821; Land Tax Assessment, Dronfield, 1816; Electoral Register, Dronfield, 1832.

3. DRO, Land Tax Assessment, Dronfield, 1818, Lichfield Joint Record Office, will of Thomas Jenkinson, 13 January 1843.

4. DRO, LTA, Dronfield, 1832.

5. See Appendix I for hatting terms.

6. Information from Mr Neil Ward, Brookside.

7. DRO, 566A/ULB 3.

8. Dronfield Henry Fanshawe School archives.

9. DRO, Whittington and Dronfield registers; Dronfield LTA, 1780-1832; *White's Directory of Sheffield and District,* 1852.

10. DRO, JWC, letter 1 Dec. 1834.

11. *Sheffield Iris,* 20 June 1809, advertisement for Joseph Taylor's academy, and passim for house sales.

12. DRO, JWC, letter, 9 Aug. 1834.

13. J. Palmer, *A Short History of Dronfield Independent Church*, 1934.

14. DRO, JWC, letter, 25 Aug. 1833.

15. Lucas's remained an important part of the Dronfield industrial scene for 160 years after the acquisition of the foundry site. The final castings were produced on 24 Dec. 1971.

16. Dronfield Town Council, deed to former Dronfield UDC estate (Council Offices, Church Street).

17. Ebenezer Elliott, 1781-1849, had a small iron merchant's business in Sheffield in the 1820s and 1830s; he was active in the agitation for political reform and also well known in literary circles. His *Corn Law Rhymes*, born of his hatred of what he called 'the bread tax', appeared in 1831 and met with much popular success; they painted a vivid picture of life as it was for the poor, blaming all their ills on the operation of the Corn Laws *(Dictionary of National Biography)*.

18. *The Derbyshire Patriot*, of which there are copies in Derby Local Studies Library, was published weekly from May 1833 by Thomas Ford, Chesterfield. The 'Buckingham Review' is probably the *Parliamentary Review*, published by J.S. Buckingham, M.P. for the new borough of Sheffield in the Reform Parliament of 1832; he sat until 1837 and was especially interested in social reform and the temperance movement. The proposed publication of the *Parliamentary Review* is referred to in the *Sheffield Iris*, 15 Jan. 1833. The 'Lodge' was a local branch of the Oddfellows, Manchester Unity Friendly Society, which met at the Red Lion.

19. Carver Street Chapel, built 1804, was known as the Methodist Cathedral of Sheffield *(Methodist Conference Handbook, 1922)*; the Methodist New Connexion had chapels in Scotland Street and South Street (the old name for the Moor), the latter built in 1828. Dawson and Bunting preached Methodist missionary sermons at both Carver Street and Ebenezer Chapel, Moorfields, on Sunday, Monday and Tuesday, 21-23 April 1833 *(Sheffield Iris, 16 April 1833)*.

20. DRO, JWC, letter, 15 March 1833.

21. DRO, Land Tax Assessment, Dronfield, 1832.

22. Calvin Colton, *Manual for Emigrants to America*, 1832; Colton was the author of many books on America.

23. DRO, JWC, letter, 21 Sept. 1840.

24. Ibid., 8 Oct. 1854.

25. Diary, 5 Jan. 1843; it is possible that E.C. was Elizabeth, daughter of the Rev. David Clark.

26. On 8 Jan. 1843 Joseph wrote 'Mt. St.' instead of the usual 'M. . . St'; the assumption is that 'Mt.' is Mount.

27. New workmen were required to pay a 'footing' or fine, called a garnish in the hatting trade, and generally spent on drink. Parsons was probably a new workmate.

28. DRO, Dronfield parish register.

29. DRO, JWC, letter, 30 Sept. 1848.

30. Ibid., 25 Aug. 1833, 5 and 7 April 1833, 9 Aug. 1834, 1 Dec. 1834.

28

31. Forbes Dobb was head of the grammar school at Dickinson College, Carlisle, Pennsylvania, but was dismissed for using undue force to punish a student for lateness (information kindly provided by Miss Martha Slotten of Dickinson College Library).

32. Census enumerator's book, St Saviour's, Southwark, 1841.

33. DRO, JWC, letter, 30 Oct. 1840.

34. Information from Southwark Local Studies Library.

35. See Appendix II for hatting firms.

36. Information from Dr J.H. Smith, Manchester University Extra-Mural Dept.

37. An Independent Church situated between 4 and 5 Union Street, Southwark.

38. Surrey Zoological Gardens, Manor Place, Walworth, was formed by a Mr Cross, 1831-2; an advertisement in *The Times*, 4 Sept. 1839, promised 'Grand Promenades Musicales et Champetres - Exhibitions of Mr H. Carter's extraordinary newly developed light, Konisphostic, and eruptions of Mount Hecla . . .'. Astley's Royal Amphitheatre, Westminster Bridge Road, was established by the eccentric Philip Astley c.1774 as an open riding school; between pit and stage there was a circular ride featuring 'extraordinary performances from talented male and female performers' (*London as it is today: Where to go and what to see, during the Great Exhibition*, 1851).

39. British and American Steam Navigation Company's steam ship *British Queen*, 2,016 tons, 500 h.p., Lieut. Richard Roberts R.N., master. She was intended to leave Gravesend the first day of each month and Portsmouth the following day. This was her second voyage. Advertisement in *The Times*, 29 Aug. 1839.

40. DRO, JWC.

41. i.e. the Duke of Cumberland, brother of William IV, who succeeded as Elector of Hanover in 1837, since the rule of succession prevented the accession of Queen Victoria (E.L. Woodward, *The Age of Reform 1815-1870*, Oxford, 1962, pp. 101-2).

42. The election was a very rowdy affair. The Radicals were called violent bullies and the loudest bawlers for Liberalism. Southwark was said to be in the hands of barefaced demagogues. *The Times*, 24 Jan. 1840.

43. Ibid., in commenting on the election of Wood, called him an ultra-Radical or revolutionary and said that the constituents of Southwark would have time to repent. Tennyson d'Eyncourt was the younger brother of George Tennyson, an uncle of the poet. Joseph Hume, 1777-1855, was born in Montreal, worked as a surgeon in India, 1800-1807, M.P. 1812; a philosophical radical who helped to draw up the basic Chartist document in 1838. 'Mr Byng' is probably either Sir John Byng (1772-1860), M.P. for Poole and a supporter of the Reform Bill, or his brother George Byng (1764-1847), M.P. for Middlesex.

44. Rattening was sabotage carried out by groups of workmen against employers, machinery and even fellow workmen; it was widely practised in Sheffield and north-east Derbyshire.

45. There was a hatmaker named I.Q. Harris in Winchester Place, Union Street, Southwark, at this time. Harris had also been M.P. for Southwark: *Morning Chronicle*, 6 Oct. 1839.

46. One of the more inflammatory speakers for the Anti-Corn Law League, dismissed in 1846 when it became obvious that Peel had been converted to the League's cause. Falvey also addressed a meeting in Southwark on 16 Jan. 1843, making what was described as a powerful speech. *Morning Chronicle,* 16 Jan. 1843.

47. William and Thomas Baxter kept the Marquis of Granby public house: Southwark Libraries, Clink No. 5 Ratebook, 1839.

48. O'Connor was the 'lion', the king of Chartism, a man with great popular appeal. He became obsessed with the idea of land reform and spoke on it at the Birmingham Convention of September 1839.

49. The monument stands at the junction of High St and what is now the Civic Centre; as well as commemorating Peel's death in 1850, the structure also housed the town pump. It was erected in 1854 by public subscription at a cost of £52, most of the committee being men who had shared Joseph's youthful political leanings.

50. It has not been possible to trace an Embleton in Clapham; a Luke Embleton, an engineer aged 45-49 in 1841, lived in New Park St, Southwark, between 1838 and 1846: census enumerator's book and ratebook, St Saviour's parish.

51. DRO, JWC, letter, 19 Oct. 1844.

52. *Water Witch* was one of the Humber Steam Company's 'fast and superior steamships', Capt. N. Gibson, master; she left St Katherine's Steam Wharf with goods and passengers on Tuesdays at 8 a.m.; saloon fare 10s, bed 2s, fore-cabin 3s; passengers usually arrived in Yorkshire and Lincolnshire on Wednesdays. *The Times,* 23 Sep. 1839.

53. No information regarding this affair has been discovered; the assumption is that Irwin was declared bankrupt; Joseph Jenkinson was sharing a house in Redcross St with a T. Irwin from Sept. 1845 to March 1846 (St Saviour's parish ratebooks) but it is not known whether this was his former employer.

54. DRO, JWC, letter, 30 Oct. 1840.

55. Lichfield JRO, Will of Thomas Jenkinson, dated Jan. 1843, proved 12 Oct. 1843.

56. DRO, JWC, letter, 30 Sept. 1848.

57. Sheffield City Library, Newspaper Cuttings relating to Sheffield, Vol. 25, p. 48; DRO, Railway Plan 147; 1851 Census.

58. See local directories and census enumerator's books for Dronfield, 1861-81.

59. DRO, JWC, letters, 22 May 1848, 19 Dec. 1851; *Post Office Street Directory of London,* 1852, and Thomas Jenkinson's account book (note 8).

60. In the possession of Miss Jennings, Lea Road, Dronfield.

61. DRO, JWC, Joseph Jenkinson's funeral bill.

The Diary of Joseph Jenkinson

Part I

IN ACCORDANCE with the recommendations of Mr. Cobbett, in his 'advice to a young man'[1] I have several times thought of keeping a journal wherein to insert every particular transaction or occurrence; but have found that 'procrastination is the thief of time' have always found when I should have carried my design into execution some business to prevent me doing it or some excuse which *seemed to* justify me in not doing it. Have long been convinced of the utility nay even of the necessity of something of this kind so that a person might look back upon the time he had spent, and ask in the language of the Pythegorean[2]

> 'Where have my feet chose out their way?'
> 'What have I learnt wherein I've been'
> 'From all I've heard, from all I've seen
> 'What know I more thats worth the knowing?'
> 'What have I done thats worth the doing?
> 'What have I sought that I should shun?'
> 'What duty have I left undone?'
> 'Or into what new follies run?'

I believe another great advantage likely to result from such an undertaking to be the easy reference to any particular occurrence for by its being there inserted at the time it occurs it may be referred to at any period, however distant; the remembrance of it is thereby rendered safe and sure and the mind is disburdened of many little subjects which might obstruct its progress in greater ones: — when the mind is continually occupied with every trivial occurrence (some of which would even be of importance at a future time) it is like a person who keeps tasting everything that comes in his way and can never make a hearty meal in consequence; he is fill'd up with little things and cannot receive any substantial fare. I have also several other reasons for commencing the present undertaking (all of which I have not time to mention) but one is the contracting a habit for business, and employing a leisure hour for profit and amusement: another and not the least is I was rather unjust upon a particular friend in requesting him to commence a similar work and think it would be very imprudent and inconsistent in one to wish to impose upon another person a task I was unwilling to undertake myself and not to avail myself of the advantages which I assured him I believed would result from the work feeling satisfied that these and many other benefits will arise from it and that the pleasure and the profit will suffice for the labor and the pains employ'd, I have deliberately resolved to proceed with the work upon the following plan viz. in the 1st place to enter several particular things which are fresh in my recollection and to which I can give the proper date. 2ndly to make a minute every evening of the most particular events of the day to commence on the 1st of May - 3rdly to make notes of any very important matter I may meet with in reading; anything particularly interesting or anything likely to be eventually useful.

April 16 - 1833   The family of Mr. Dobb[3] took their departure from Dronfield to go to America consisting of Mrs. and 6 children. I accompanied them to Sheffield for the purpose of bringing back the conveyance they all going together in Mr. E. Lucas' carriage.

April 17 - 1833   Robt. Lee, Thos Jenkinson and myself went to the Swan to take a farewell of Mr. Dobb - who left Dronfield that evening by the Telegraph coach for America.

April 21 Sunday   Went to Sheffield in company with my Brother David to hear the 'Methodist Missionary Sermons'[4] preached, went to Ebenezer Chapel[5] in the forenoon where we heard the Rev'd Jabez Bunting[6] from the . . . of . . . 'O Israel thou shalt not be forgotten of me', the Preacher illustrated the text very beautifully by showing that the promise included all who believed on the Lord, and that most of the other scriptural promises were liable to the construction, confirming his assertions by the works of the Apostles - his manner was masterly and elegant but to me there appeared a want of feeling throughout the whole of the delivery nor did I find that depth of reasoning nor closeness of application which I expected, there seemed a want of energy:— In the afternoon we heard Mr. Dawson[7] of Carver Street Chapel[8] from 32 - Exodus 26 Verse 'Who is on the Lord's side! let him come unto me, - The preacher is an elderly man quite plain appearance rather eccentric in his manner of preaching - but very much calculated to make strong impressions which I believe the present Sermon did on an extremely great congregation the chapel being crowded to excess. He made a beautiful allusion to the genealogy of Moses, whom he characterised as a 'most remarkable man, descending from a most remarkable family and appointed to a most remarkable business - after a humorous but very appropriate introduction he proceeded to illustrate the subject, in the 1st place by a 'careful examination and 2nd. 'by a respectful invitation, in the course of the examination he made all his conclusions by asking the question 'Who is on the Lords side' and one man in the height of his enthusiasm loudly vociferated 'I am' at which the preacher appeared astounded but prettily replied 'The Lord increase the number':— one part of the examination was I think calculated to have *particular* effect it was in the form of a dialogue between the preacher and a converted sinner in the which he asked how he knew he was on the Lords side, answered by giving the experience of a person who had left all his iniquitous practices described his feelings told how it was he felt -- that he was on the Lords side, pointed out the many advantages (spiritual and temporal) in being on that side, and in a truly rustic manner supposed the following occurrence and

32

he here apologised to the congregation saying his simile might be deemed improper for the pulpit but though most desirous not to say anything to disgrace the profession he hoped this plain tale in his plain way would not be unacceptable:— suppose a person went into a smiths shop and there saw a journeyman at work, he asks what he is doing he is answered by the man 'I am making a chain, he goes several days successively tells the man he works very hard, always finding him at the same work but he one day goes and says 'Well my man you are at your old work I see!' - 'Yes sir and a very hard job I have on't' - 'What wages do your master give you!' 'He has never given me anything yet but he promises fair what he'll do' - 'Do you know what that chain's for?' 'No' 'But I will tell you When you have completed it - *it is to bind you fast in for ever and ever*:— at hearing this he said 'Down goes the hammer':— saying I'll never make another link for him while I live - O sinner said he hear this intelligence! thou art working for the same master he will give thee the same wages - every sin thou commits adds one more link to the chain, take pattern by the one I have mentioned leave his service and enter thou into the service of Jesus Christ who will reward thee for thy labour with ever-lasting happiness' this is the substance of the simile which with his peculiar style of delivery made a very strong impression on the audience (and I trust on the individual who was so happy in hearing him and is now penning this homeley account of him) he also alluded to Mr. Fletcher preaching once at Leeds and describing himself as a recruiting officer in the army of the Lord Jesus Christ in which capacity *he himself* was then acting - he concluded by earnestly entreating us all to join some regiment and said he did not mind which it was provided we were in the service - my time will not allow of more being said but hope it was *a never to be forgotton sermon.* Went to see Will'm Dalton after tea, found him considerably better than when I saw him before; he walked on with me to the River Sheaf as did also his father (whom I find a very intelligent man and was much delighted with his company) - and a Mr. Belcher whose brother-in-law a Mr. Wheatcroft was just gone to America with his wife and family - left them a little after 6 o'clock and had a very pleasant walk home with my Brother and Mr. Schofield who I met with at Ebenezer Chapel in the forenoon, and had been with him all the time since.

April 28th. Sunday Arose early in the morning - spent the forenoon in reading went with Wm Slack to see Josh Coope who I was sorry to find very much worse than when I last saw him, never saw any one to the best of my knowledge more altered in so short a time he lay in bed and had the appearance of *Death* - he spoke of the probability of a short period of time being allowed him in this world with great complacency - he was very much oppressed with pain a short time before we arrived so much so that his mother thought he would have terminated his existence at the time -

April 29   Went to work at my Uncles they wanting to send a few Dozens of proofs off immediately and had nobody to assist them, it was more than 12 months since I had been in the shop before because I considered myself ill treated when I worked for him and did not think well to go near them - though I bore no malice on account of it *not the least* but thought I would 'Keep away' till I was asked to go:— which I did.

April 30   Saw the Sheffd Iris paper[9] - and in it the report of a Division in the house of Commons on a motion of Sir W. Ingilby[10]   for 'reducing or repealing the Malt Tax' [11]   in which the Ministers were in the minority by 10. This was hailed throughout the country as an omen of something being done for the people - Lord Althorp[12]   having said the week before they could not spare the malt duty - so the general opinion was that the members would work for the country not for the Ministry any longer.

May 1st. 1833 Wednesday   Went to work about 6 in the morning at my Uncles came to dinner and was much surprised to find Josh Makinson sat; - had not seen him of a long time, he had just come from Spilsby in Lincolnshire, went to Earnshaws sent for Tom; we talk'd seriously to him concerning his rambling habits, he promised to refrain them, and added he was tired of running through the country - said he did not fear getting work anywhere and would turn his back on no man he went forward to Sheffield same night - turned out a very wet evening.

May 2nd Thursday   A warm day - left work at my Uncles and nigh rolled off 6 stuff hats at home (which were wanted) went to Earnshaw to seek Tom at night to go with me to Woodhouse found him rather tipsy with drinking Parsons' garnish[13] - left him and engag'd G. Seston to go the following day -

May 3   Work'd very closely all day and at night my hands were sorer than I have known them for many months - having roll'd very near 9 hats - staid in the shop while nearly 10 o'clock and then left my Uncle at work.

May 4   A very fine day - went to work at my Uncles again at ½ past 4 in the morning staid 'till 7 o'clock Ill when I finished my work - went to the Lodge[14] spent a very comfortable evening - saw Buckingham Review[15]   after I left the Lodge I was thunder-struck to see that Sir W Ingilby's motion was rescinded by a motion of Lord Althorps - to that effect and that Sir J. Key's[16] motion for the repeal of the house & Window Tax be rejected was carried by a great majority - I think 355 - 131 - thought all was over.

May 5 Sunday   Arose early - the brightness of the sun, the sweetness of the breeze and the melody of the birds, gave a pressing invitation to walk out for to enjoy them - Whilst hesitating on the subject Geo Ward and my cousin Tom came and we went together into the Manor [17] garden - and while looking at the ruinous old building (the Halls) was led to contemplate on the bygone days - when that was the residence of a family to whom the villagers looked as their patrons & protectors - whose bounteous hand was ne'er withheld, whenever their necessities required its aid, who had learnt to estimate their poorer neighbours as fellow creatures and by a constant residence amongst them - and a cultivation of reciprocal good feeling they lived together in the greatest harmony compared with the present day - when the whole presents a scene such as novelists paint in the height of their romantic ideas, *complete desolation* seems to rule supreme the front garden may be said to resemble the one in the 'Country clergyman' [18] 'A few torn shrubs the place disclose' - but on approaching the porch of the Hall the eye seems to shrink from the spectacle - in that place where many a rustic friend has met a hearty welcome is seen the miserable remains of an old bell pull - the seats which by the Squire were oft adorned, are now grown o'er with moss - and the floor and steps - which often the housemaids pride did raise to see them neat and clean, are now all green and damp and every joint thickset with grass but where are now the owners? changed from the great race, whom virtue made so truly noble to what the flatt'ring world does call 'a Lady' - whom *charity* nor *virtue* knows but who to screen the *faults* she'll not avoid has taken shelter in the bustle of the Town, where with the man her lust hath chose she spends the wealth from this *poor* village drawn to gratify the worst of passions nor heeds nor knows how fare the poor from who that wealth was wrung. But here my contemplation met a check, the village bells announced that it was 8 and summoned away to take a plain repast and prepare for holier duty.

Was a few minutes too late at school [19] by which I incurred the penalty of a penny - did not complain of that because I'd had a voice in making the law by which it was impos'd went to Chapel [20] in the forenoon and heard a sermon from 11 verse of the 9 chapter of the Acts ('And the Lord said unto him, arise, and go into the street which is called Straight and inquire in the house of Judas for one called Saul of Tarsus for behold he prayeth') by a strange person who came to supply Mr. Clarke he being gone to supply Mr. Larcum [21] of Sheffield - Dined, went again to school and entered upon the services which I found more arduous than before, carelessness had took possession of most of the boys and after several attempts to restrain them without success I being left with only J. Gratton to assist me found it necessary to suspend the proceedings and to call their attention to a few observations I had to make to them lectured them rather severely call'd their attention to the deep state of ignorance in which many of them were found the many evils consequent upon it:— the opportunities they had of extricating themselves from it, the kindness of their benefactors the sacrifices of the teachers the comparative advantages of knowledge over ignorance their great abuse of these favours and an earnest solicitation to abandon their follies and betake themselves to that which was likely to be of such permanent utility, and to avail themselves of the opportunities they had afforded of receiving a pious education, though the discourse was homely - I trust it had a good effect - delivered it in very familiar language and sincerely hope it will be useful - after which the preacher addressed a few words to the scholars (the service having concluded in the interim) great attention was paid during singing and prayer and an evident improvement was manifested . . . Took tea - delivered a lecture at the Lodge. Went to see Josh Coope did not see him but was told he was worse - saw John who had just arrived from Bolton found him in good trim but not much different in other respects:— staid till past 9 o'clock then returned home sup'd, retired to my humble couch to enjoy that repose which the labour of the day so loudly call'd for. Thank'd a Kind Providence for sustaining me & pray'd for support for the future.

May 6 Monday   Well refreshed with the past nights sleep cheerfully commenced the labour of another week about 6 in the morn continued till about 7 in the evening - work'd after tea at my uncles to part roll and block 3 of our own hats -

May 7 Tuesday   Sent 29 stuff hats to Mr Booths [22] - heard the Iris Paper read by Tom, find the country is much agitated at the conduct of ministers, meetings held in various parts of the Kingdom particularly in London, strong language used at them all the ministers are openly denounced as traitors - Birmingham speak openly of resistance to taxes, recommend the people to 'be prepared to help themselves' - for say they the parliament will do nothing for you.[23] Sir J. Hobhouse [24]   has resigned his office as Sec for Ireland - and his seat for West-[minst] er being pledg'd to vote against the house & taxes and the Min[ister] s were for supporting them (strange confusion!)

May 9 Wednesday   Rose rather early wrote to [*Blank*] went to post, paid postage - returned to work work'd all day and at night retired with the satisfaction that by the 'sweat of my brow I had earned my bread' (for *I had* sweat the day being very warm)

May 9   Not up so early quite as usual - think I was indolent. breakfasted and got to work about 7 went down to my Uncles to wet off some hats - got in the sunshine which was very hot - and found some difficulty in quitting it commenc'd work in good earnest in the forenoon and made 4 light bodies - a rather severe thunder storm P.M. accompanied by heavy rain continued several hours at intervals - the vegetable kingdom soon evinc'd the benefits it had receiv'd from the refreshing showers.

May 10 Friday   Went in the evening to Woodhouse & Holmesfield in company with G. Seston, J. Platts & my cousin Tom, the latter of whom had to visit the sick belonging to the benefit society call'd at Hydes' had a pint of ale each - jok'd a little about Dronfield milk which Tom said 'look'd like th' sky round th' side of a basin:— had a very pleasant walk home - went to bed between 10 to 11.

May 11 Saturday   M. Flint called on me, rec'd a note from Jas. Fowler after tea. Mr. Hollingworth called at the shop as he said to see me not having seen me for so long - heard from him that Mr. Dobb sail'd at the time he spoke of going by a vessel call'd the Napolean, said Mr. Ward had told him, he did not like the state of the political world - we had each seen the *Derbyshire Patriot* [25] (I for the first time) of that day - Westminster election came on Wedensday the people would not hear Hobhouse speak but pelted him with vegetables, mud or anything of the kind they could lay hold of: his opponents were Wm Escott - a Tory - & Col Evans a Radical,[26]   the show of hands decidedly for the Col. but the others demanded a poll, heard in the evening that Evans headed the poll 200 work'd 'till 9 o'clock having had 8 bodies to make that day to send off in the morning - sent to Earnshaws for a pint of ale; reckon'd for 26 bodies & went to bed

May 12 - Sunday   Occupied the early part of the morning in a manner not at all suited to my feelings - but which I was obliged to do as part of my business - viz to send off some goods to London they not being dry to pack up on the Saty night - took a slight aperient my custom in the spring to regulate the blood - read in the forenoon - after dinner walk'd out with G. Wd who had just recovered from an attack of the Influenza (which is very prevelent just now - many families are *wholly* afflicted - Mr. Butterman has had 25 out of about 30 pupils ill at the same time) - I read the life of Paley[27]   in the fields dont much approve his conduct think he was very ambitious - went in the evening to Chapel where we had a very serious discourse from the 17 C[hapter] of the gospel by John 17 verse 'Sanctify them through thy truth, thy word is truth' - returning from chapel - found myself warmly thank'd by Mr. Ward concerning Mr. Dobbs affairs for which I was totally unprepared not thinking the brute (who had also been at Chapel) could have so soon forgot the service - although I had rec'd intimations that he intended to do it, gave him to understand I was fully prepar'd for him when there should be a fitting opportunity.

May 13   Went to work by 6 o'clock remain'd there till tea time a hot day went with E. Allen to the Swan to see a London paper, saw one and learnt from it that Col Evans was return'd for West[minster] by a majority of 188 a sad shock to the ministry - Bells[28] in noticing this says 'the last recommendation the Col. had was that he was the 'Radicals' Wellington' the man to do the red coat work of their own part' heard from Mr. Porter that Mr. D. sail'd on the 24 all in good health & spirits.

May 14 Tuesday   A note from E. Joell heard also of E.N. being a very hot day but nothing of particular importance.

May 15 Wednesday   Rec'd a visit from Tom who was attack'd with the influenza followed immediately by one from Earnshaw in a similar situation work'd all day in the evening was visited by Wm Camm & Geo. Seston to the latter of whom I lent 'Watts' Improvement on the Mind'.[29] Read part of 'Corn Law Rhymes'[30] to my friends G. Ward was then added to the number - staid up till 11 o'clock.

May 16 Thursday   Saw Mr Wd in the afternoon I was in company with S Lucas by the side of his dam, wanted to speak to him but he went past quite sulky hardly speaking to S who was to begin the subject - work'd till near 7 o'clock when went to the preaching - heard a beautiful exhortation from [*Blank*] 'Trust ye in the Lord *for in the Lord* is everlasting strength' saw Mr. Clarke after service who kindly promis'd to lend me 'Coltons Emigrants Guide'[31]   on which he passes a high encomium found him very much disappointed at the ministerial measures for emancipating the slaves which I think all good must be - went home and found myself considerably indisposed in consequence I suppose of the imprudent step I had taken in going to a cool Chapel immediately on leaving the warm shop.

May 17 Friday   Rather unwell in the morning - work'd in great distress - suffering very much from the effects of a violent cold had a severe pain in my head - could not eat anything but was bent on finishing my work which I did betwixt 7 & 8 o'clock went home got some gruel immediately and went to bed hoping I should be better in the morning - a thunder storm in the afternoon with heavy rain.

May 18 Saty   Had very little rest the previous night was very much indisposed and did not rise till about 8 o'clock was too ill to work although I was much inclined ate nothing until afternoon got a little then & went to bed got up again about 4 o'clock was not better - soon went to bed again where I laid till 7 could not attend the Lodge - Before I went to bed heard the confirmation of a report that had several days been in circulation of a most brutal and ferocious attack being made upon a peaceable meeting of the inhabitants of London by the 'military police' without the least insult or provocation on the part of the people the police were accompanied or rather commanded by Lord Melbourne & the city magistrates who were in a room near the place of meeting (Cold bath field)[32]   the police commenc'd the attack without giving the least notice by knocking down men, women & children indiscrimately not attempting to apprehend any one but the chairman a Mr Mee for a considerable time he has for the present escaped, there were 3000 police present - they blockaded all the avenues leading from the place that none might escape one policeman was kill'd by a joiner nam'd Fursey who acted nobly in his own defence he was apprehended.

Sunday May 19   Felt a little better but could not attend to my regular duties at School but got my Bror David to officiate me nor could I attend Divine Service any part of the day went to school after the afternoon service to assist in dismissing the Scholars - saw Mr Clarke after evening service - he having told Geo. Jackson to request me to wait on him, he lent me the work he had promised me - returned home and clos'd another Sabbath *here* - rather unwell but perhaps a little better than I was in the morning.

May 20 Monday   Still unwell - work'd about an hour in the afternoon but was oblig'd to desist could not do anything to speak of - got supper of my usual diet (gruel) and again retired to rest had in the course of the day read a good deal of 'Colton's work' with which I was very much delighted - Serving as it did to encourage me in the Resolutions I had come to and holding out so reasonable a prospect for my Friend, concluded it after I got to bed - very well satisfied.

May 21 Tuesday   A little better commenc'd work but soon after relinquished it - some work arriving in the afternoon with an other for some we had in hand - my Father being very ill of the Influenza I was oblig'd to recommence work made about 3 in the day in great troubles, a pain at my stomach was so intense that I was frequently oblig'd to pause at work, and rest a short time my mother was now violently attack'd with the same complaint

May 22 Wednesday   my Parents both very ill, myself far from being well but began work to complete some to send off was much afflicted with a pain at my stomach - a legacy of the Influenza - work till about 8 when I finish'd my job - got my gruel & went to bed.

May 23 Thursday   Sent off a pack to London work'd about an hour in the forenoon but in consequence of the severity of the pain at stomach I lay down after dinner began work again about 3 P M and continued till 8 made 2 bodies, in the evening my pain was considerably abated & on the whole had as I thought sufficient reason to expect I should be able to resume my work on the morrow, and proceed in my usual course.

Here I am oblig'd to depart from the original plan several days severe illness having prevented me making minutes every evening so that I must note all that I can from memory.

May 24 Friday   Arose betwixt 6 & 7 not feeling well thought I would break-fast before I went to work as I had a severe pain in my head - the pain increas'd during the forenoon so much that my forehead over my right eye was much

39

swollen and inflam'd - went down to Mr. Nicholson who recommended a speedy application of leeches - had 5 applied in the afternoon when from the loss of blood & the acuteness of the pain I swooned away - experienced very little relief that day - went to bed when I had ceased to bleed but was a long time before I could enjoy the sweets of sleep which to me felt so desirable.

May 25 Saturday　Spent a turbulent night and 'ere I arose my ear was smote by a death-bell which upon enquiry I found announced the death of Josh Coope which happened about 1 A M was not at all surprised for when I saw him on the Monday previous I rather wondered how life could be sustained in such a feeble frame - I raised him from the bed he was 'literally speaking' a mere skeleton. Here was a subject meet for reflection - a young man of my own age who only a few months previous could boast of never having any bodily affliction and to all human appearance was likely to enjoy a much longer term of probation, summon'd to that world 'whence no trav'ler returns' there to account for all the deeds done in this life & to receive judgement accordingly - these thoughts with those of many a scene in our boyish days - impos'd themselves upon me almost instantaneously but my poor head could not entertain them, so dispers'd them as well as I could humbly praying when the summons came for myself I might be prepar'd to obey it. Rose about 9 my right eye had suffered so much from the pain in my forehead that I could not bear the rays of light and was oblig'd to keep it cover'd all day. Spent the day chiefly in bed and in taking gruel was considerably reliev'd in the evening by the company of several friends who brought the Political news of the day which was of rather peculiar nature. The jury who sat on the body of Cully the policeman (who was kill'd at Cold bath fields) after several days patient & laborious investigation during which they examined a great number of highly respectable witnesses brought in their verdict - which as it is said to be the most honest verdict ever agreed to by a jury in a similar case I will here transcribe it 'We find a verdict of *Justifiable Homicide* on these grounds, that no riot act was read nor any proclamation advising the people to disperse. That the government did not take the proper precautions to prevent the meeting from assembling and that the conduct of the police was ferocious, brutal and unprovoked by the people and we moreover express our anxious hope that government will in future take better precautions to prevent the recurrance of such disgraceful transactions in the metropolis.' The coroner refused the verdict and attempted to intimidate the jury but they remained inflexible saying - 'Before God and our country - on our solemn oaths we have given the subject all the consideration in our power and the paper we have handed to you contains the judgement on which we are unanimously agreed.' After several attempts to alter the verdict the Coroner was ultimately oblig'd to accept it.[33]　Also of a meeting in Birmingham consisting of 150 thousand people it was addressed by Mr Atwood[34]　who charg'd ministers with violating their pledges given to him and the time when the power of the Unions was so necessary to keep them in office 'They then told him that *his* duty would be when a member of Parliament to inquire into the distress of the country ', which they now denied Mr. O'Connel[35] also address'd the meeting in a very powerful & energetic manner, charging ministers as Mr. Atwood had done with their ingratitude to the people. he said 'it was the great meeting at Birmingham that carried the Reform Bill not Lords Grey & Althorp he thanked them for the Bill though the first measure of the Reform Parliament was tyranny towards Ireland he advised them to act so as not to put themselves in the power of their enemies saying. Oh! how glad the brutal ministers would be if the people violated the law Persevere! let the whole of the Kingdom cry unto the Sovereign to dismiss those 'brutal & bloody' ministers - he passed a severe sarcasm on the Whig press, which is now so full of vituperation against the Assemblies of the people he condemned the 'Corn Laws' in no measured terms as did also Mr. Atwood, call'd Lord Brougham[36] a great humbug, denounced the government plan respecting negro slavery as a trick. & delusion & concluded saying that with honest ministers the Reform Bill would give cheap government, cheap religion and above all cheap bread - on Mr. O'Connell taking his leave three hearty cheers were given for him. A petition to his Majesty was then agreed upon, calling upon him 'to dismiss his present ministers' and 'to give his royal confidence to no man who is not determined to adopt prompt, decisive and efficient measures to accomplish the restoration of the national prosperity and who does not deem it the first duty of a statesman to secure to honest industry its just reward', the meeting which continued 7 hours separated peacably. - After hearing the news retired to bed somewhat easier than I had been the greater part of the day.

Sunday May 26· Very ill in the morning got up in the forenoon was oblig'd to go to bed again after dinner was visited in the afternoon by a many friends for whose kindness I was very thankful. Arose after tea to enjoy a change of position, if not some relief my head was still very bad staid up awhile with Mark Joell, Mark Havenhand & Geo Ward who had kindly call'd upon me went to bed again I thought a little better.

Monday 27 Very unwell still spent part of the day with Samuel Ward who was very lame in his foot. improv'd considerably in the course of the day

Tuesday May 28th Was very much better in the morning, saw the procession of the 'Female Sick Society'[37] went according to invitation to Josh Coopes Funeral as might be expected I witness'd the excessive grief of a widowed mother whose greatest earthly hope was fled. Surrounded by a mournful group of children weeping bitterly for the loss of him to whom they had been taught to look as their guardian & protector, I felt my pain was gradually dimmishing & in the evening retired to rest a great deal better.

Wedensday 29 Nothing of importance happened myself was still better spent a weary day because I could not read, my illness had so affected my eyes.

Thursday May 30 Got up rather early but soon discovered by weakness & consequent inability to work although I was almost free from pain; skulk'd about the garden & in Samuel Wards' most of the day, tow'ds evening went to my Uncles Shop from thence to the house where I took tea and staid 'till past 8 o'clock, and was never suffer'd to go to sleep all the time

Friday May 31 Went to Chesterfield in the afternoon & occupied 3 hours walking there was so very weak and nearly the same coming back was very much fatigued with the journey - went in the evening to Mr. Hollingworths & settled his account - smok'd a cigar - drank a glass of rum & water - came home well refresh'd & went to bed.

Saturday June 1st Was determined to work a little today though I was still very weak, however I made 2 bodies with some difficulty - went to the Club & from thence to the Lodge,[38] staid awhile came home got a good supper (for my appetite was new whetted) and again went to bed thankful that I was so shortly released from the pain which so afflicted me only the Saturday previous.

Sunday June 2nd When I arose felt very happy at being able to resume my labors at Sunday School Mr Schofield call'd to invite me to accompany him to Sheffield thought myself too weak to undertake the journey - went to school in the morning - attended service in the Chapel in the Afternoon but my flock was so careless that it required my sole attention to govern it so that I could not at all enjoy the Sermon after tea gave a Lecture - we had some refreshing rain in the evening for which our farmers had long wished, went to bed at my usual time about 10

Monday June 3 Recommenced my daily toil but was very far from being able to proceed with it as usual, having suffer'd much from my previous illness - news came of the Government having squashed the Cold bath fields verdict in the Court of Kings Bench - the country very much disturbed - general disappointment at the conduct of the ministry.

Tuesday June 4 Work'd all the day over, felt much better than before, read an important letter of Mr. E. Elliott's to the Editor of the Morning Chronicle[39] also an extract from the Parliamentary Review on the State of the public mind & the conduct of the Whigs, neither of which hesitate to say that the time is almost arriv'd for a change and both intimate that the most likely way to affect it is by *force*

Wednesday June 5 After finishing my daily labour about ½ past 7 attended a Teachers Meeting in the Vestry of the Chapel. Mr. Clarke was present and kindly offer'd to provide a feast for the Teachers & children which it was agreed to have on Tuesday in the Feast Week,[40] he also requested the married teachers to bring their wives - the single ones their female companions - and here my heart was mov'd & thoughts across my mind did rush which I wont here transcribe

Thursday June 6 Was afraid of a relapse having got a slight cold the previous evening - but was happy that my fears were groundless for after dinner was much better. Went my usual round of duty and so concluded another day.

Friday June 7 Performed the duties of another day cheerfully and comfortably - being much better qualified to work than I was in the early part of the week.

Saturday June 8 Commenced work about 6 A M and continued it till about 9 P M chatted about ½ an hour with Robert Lee at our house, reckon'd for 26 bodies. Supped and went to bed.

Sunday June 9th Prepared by early rising to enjoy the sweets of another Sabbath was waited upon by Cousin Tom according to previous arrangement to take a trip to Sheffield partly to enjoy the pleasure and (I hoped) to receive the profit of Mr. Allins' preaching fell in with Mr. Schofield. the morning was very hot - were too late for the morning service at Norfolk St [41] but just heard the conclusion of the Sermon in a solemn eloquent and energetic appeal to the audience requesting them to open the doors of their hearts to the knocking of the Saviour. Was very much struck with the whole style of preaching that I enquired of the Preacher and found that he was an Independent Gent, who had acquired his fortune by marriage, after having qualified for the Ministry - his name is Chambers - and I think he is remarkably clever. Found upon enquiry that Mr. Allens labours were for a time suspended in consequence of his ill health for the benefit of which he was going to the Isle of Man - Saw an Advertisement that Mr. *Berry* [42] was to preach at South Street on the following Sunday and at once determined (health & circumstances permitting) to hear him - went down to the Old Church [43] from thence to Scotland Street Chapel [44] to hear a Mr. Burrows - who preach'd for the first time (in Mr. Allins situation as Superintendent) from the 16 or 15 C[hapter] last verses 'Therefore, my beloved brethern, be ye steadfast, unmoveable, always abounding in the work of the Lord for as much as ye know that your labour is not in vain in the Lord.' he preach'd very well showing the cause & effect of Infidelity - the means used by some to lead ignorant Christians astray & concluded by an excellent paraphrase on his text.

Dined at my Uncles - went to Fir Vale with Tom to see his sister Ann - got home about 5 took tea went in the evening to hear Mr. Clarke who had before promised to improve the discourse to young people by a reference to the Death [of] Joseph Coope and the Female Passenger who died suddenly at the Swan - he was much depressed in spirits on account of the dangerous state of his son Joshs health who had broke a blood vessel & his life was dispaired of by the Physcicians - he preach from 'For my life is but a span - the discourse was a very affectionate one as may be expected chiefly on the uncertainty of life, the certainty of death, and the great importance of a pious life to prepare for that great change which will one day affect us all. there was a very large audience.

Monday June 10 A very fine day this - spent by me in procuring a livelihood by my usual vocation.

Tuesday June 11   Look'd over and sent off today five hats to London, commenc'd work about 11 o'clock and continued it throughout the day - till about 7.

Wedensday June 12 Concluded my work and went to bed not daring to read because of the pain in my head returning.

Thursday June 13   Did not arise till after 8 o'clock my mind was very much disturbed with thoughts that pressed upon me in the night in the form of dreams lay awake a long time my Brother Tom brought me a letter that had just come before, recognised the writing and in my eagerness to know its contents - did almost shudder fearing some accident had befallen the family of Mr. Dobb from who it had come soon discovered that the letter had been delay'd by some one it having been wrote on board the Napolean in Liverpool went in the evening to a meeting of the Sunday School Teachers, which Mr. Clarke attended and kindly proffer'd to provide a Feast for the Scholars & Teachers on the Tuesday in Dronfield Feast Week.

Friday June 14   This evening I have nothing important to record, the Political world is strangeley agitated at this time, respecting the Emancipation of the Slaves and other subjects - Mr. Gisbourne [45] made a severe attack on Mr. Stanley [46] for calling upon the House to grant 20 millions of money to the West India proprietors as a compensation without first proving injury - or giving notice of his intention to the House for the original clause was that 15 millions should be granted as a loan, the ministers however carried the amendment and thus subjected the White slaves to a payment of about 1 million per annum for only a shadow of Freedom for their black brethren in the West India. Poor Johnny Bull!

Saturday June 15   Concluded the weeks' work about 6 P M went to the Lodge [47] was appointed to the District Meeting at Castleton, staid 'till about 11 went home & to bed

Sunday June 16   Rose about ½ past 5 to prepare for a journey to Sheffield Mr. Schofield call'd upon me by the time appointed. Tom was behind time I had to go & call him up - started ¼ to 7 turn'd out very wet as we went up Sheffield Moore - went to Norfolk St Chapel and again heard a Local preacher. After service went to the White Hart, Waingate - drank 3 pints of Porter and waited while 'twas time for service at South Street, proceeded thence and was soon gratified by a sight of Mr. Berry who I thought had a very graceful appearance but what was that when compared to his service? after reading 1 Chapter of Old and another out of the New Testament he offered up one of the most solemn feeling sublime & beautiful prayers I ever heard from the lips of man, the whole tenor of his prayer indicated the liberality of his mind, no praying for governors or their measures but his whole heart was absorbed with the state of the poor & this fervent prayer was that they might be reliev'd from their distress, that the earth might be freed from oppression and tyranny - that slavery might be abolish'd and concluded his pathetic petition by the word liberty which he had before pray'd might be establish'd throughout the world. He took for his text the 21st verse 1st chapter of St Paul's first Epistle to the Corinthians 'For after that in the wisdom of God the world by wisdom knew not God, it pleased God by the foolishness of preaching to save them that believe'. If my mind had been at all prejudiced against him on account of a Sermon he had published some parts of which I did not approve 'The Rod' that feeling must immediately have left me on the Introduction to the Discourse being delivered, if it had not before been dispell'd - the substance of his argument was, *that religion being solely of a spiritual nature cannot be connected with secular affairs without being defiled.* he proved it by comparing Christianity in its first state (viz 3 first centuries) with Christianity in our day he contended for the right of Religion to support itself and completely apart all church establishments - he declared that he felt it to be a duty to oppose anything that had a tendency to obstruct the spread of Religion - the first part of his business in discussing the text was to show the insufficiency of human reasoning in matters of Divinity, he alluded to high state of human greatness that had been attained by the Greeks and many other nations before the time of Christ and with all this wisdom he clearly showed their ignorance of God, he said the wisdom of the Ancients was divided into the natural wisdom or a system of morality and Divine wisdom a knowledge of which should have made them or was supposed to have made them acquainted with the nature and attributes of the Divine Being he proved their ignorance in the knowledge of the true God in shewing their absurd notions respecting their different deities, the abmoninable practises that were suffered in their worship - and the retrograding rather than advancing of Religion amongst them - this was by depending on their own reason and not seeking the Light of Revelation, he spoke of the means adapted by God to proclaim his word, viz preaching here he severely censured any one that stood forward to display his own talents and not solely for the purpose appointed by God, which he called ostentation and vanity - but encouraged all who undertook the work from pure motives to press on to the prize of their high calling - have not time to say more but was very much delighted with the whole of the service and gave 6d (all I could afford) towards the subscription. was sorry to see such a slender congregation. Went in the afternoon to the Catholic Chapel[48] were very kindly treated but did not much like the service but am quite willing to let those enjoy it that do like it - there was a good congregation & an excellent organ, the ceremony was cold, and too much like their relative the Church of England. Tom & I came home & left Mr. S. in Sheffield to hear evening service - had scarcely got home ere I was sent for to - and was much surprised to meet Mr. W. White & Mrs and her sister, he told me they had come purposely to see me thought I was being highly honored - they did not stay very long Mr. W.s business prevented him we had a bit of a chat, and a laugh about his wedding (at which ceremony I was Father)[49] then they departed 'twixt 7 & 8, saw Mr. Davis come out of the Chapel, had not seen him for a long time 6 or 7 months, we were on very good terms and I walk'd with him to Hardys bank[50] on his way to Chesterfield. I now began to think of closing another Sabbath, so returned home to a humble but hearty repast pray'd that I might be assisted to turn what I heard to good advantage and then should I have cause to venerate the day throughout my whole life - a bad pen & no quills.

Monday June 17   Roll'd off 2 hats and went to Sheffield to a committee meeting of the District - rode in Mr. Clarks carriage to Heely Bar, business detained me till 11 o'clock bought a — for Tom slept at my Uncles.

Tuesday June 18   Breakfasted and took my departure about 9 A M call'd at my Sisters - also at Sharrow House[51] got home about 1 P M and work'd the remainder of the day.

Wedensday June 19   Work'd all day till 8 o'clock then attended a Lodge Committee and enforc'd a most painful but necessary duty viz the [*Blank*] of a member staid till past 9.

Thursday June 20   Went at 8 o'clock to a Teachers meeting that was adjourned from the Monday previous - only 2 or 3 attended suppose they were all busy preparing for the Feast

Friday June 21   All work today the women remarkable active to 'get done' for the feast work'd till about 9 came home & went to bed:— promised to write to Mr. Schofield took my Farewell this evening.

Saturday June 22   After work today was occupied till 11 P M in examining and packing 9 Doz stuff bodies to send off the following morning - my Uncle

Taylor came in the evening had sent a letter to him that morning by Mr Schofield also one to [*Blank*].

Sunday June 23 This morning was by many in our village hail'd with joy in the expectation of meeting with some friend or relation who usually made an annual visit - this was the case at our house for Aunt Slack, Thos and some of the little ones came also my Uncle Josh all of whom we were glad to see and though no advocate for Feasts I thought they were of some utility in bringing together Friends who may perhaps reside a long way distant and would more seldom see each other were it not for these occasions though I must admit they are frequently turned to worse purposes some as it were seem to think they are licensed to commit all kind of excesses to get drunk, fight, and to be put under no restraint and the idle plea for all this is 'its Feast' surely we can do as we like today - went to the Chapel in Forenoon heard 18th Chapter of Genesis illustrated by Mr. Clarke which he did by a reference to ancient history and a description of the manners of the Eastern nations then & at the present, which he considered necessary to meet the opponent of Religion, who ridicule the idea of Sarah making the cakes and cooking a calf for only 3 men & he said that calves in that part of the world were a great deal less than ours, and such is the hospitality of the Asiatics even at the present day that they give away meat & drink to every one who calls on them (a calf weighs about 14 lbs) after hearing an excellent discourse went home partook of an excellent dinner, went to school after afternoons' service, could not attend chapel in the evening at which I was much grieved.

Monday June 24 [*No further entries*]

Part II

1839 September 1st Sunday Yesterday Saturday about 8 A M was very greatly surprised by the arrival of Mr Edward Hoyle of Oldham [52] and his sister a young lady of about 14 - they had come from Liverpool by Railway having left there at 7 P M Friday and had breakfasted at the Bull & Mouth previous to their calling on me. I accompanied them to the office of the 'British Queen Steamer' [53] (No 4 Fen Court, Fen Church St) by which vessel they were to proceed to New York fare for Adults 40 Guineas Fore Cabin; 50 Guineas aft. came home at 9 A M attended to business till 2 P M when with Mr. Irwins' permission I went over to the Bull & Mouth to see him (Mr. Irwin) start on his journey and also to see Mr. Hoyle - had 2 glasses of Brandy & water with Mr I and then set out with Mr H & his Sister to as many of the publick sights as our

DRONFIE

from the Inc

Key

1. Luke Jenkinson's house.
2. Thomas Jenkinson's house.
3. Workshop.
4. Independent church.
5. White Swan Inn.
6. Red Lion Inn.
7. Green Dragon Inn.

8. Parish ch
9. Vicarage
10. Old Gra
11. Taylor's
12. Butterm
13. Manor F
14. Wreakes
15. Vale Ho

GREEN LANE

CALLEYWHITE LANE

19

LEA LANE

MILL LANE

Dam 23

TO 22

18   17   23

5

RIVER DRONE

TO CHESTERFIELD →

QUOIT
GREEN

HALLOWES LANE

IN 1846

re Award

School.

hool.

16.	Lucas works and dam.
17.	Damstead works.
18.	Damstead House.
19.	Cliffe House.
20.	Usher's house (Red House).
21.	Blue Posts (Stoops).
22.	Chemical manufactory.
23.	Dronfield corn mill and dam.

limited time would allow us to visit St Pauls, Westminster Abbey, Buckingham Palace, Whitehall the Horse Guards, Regent St, Piccadilly, Hyde Park etc etc the weather was very unfavorable but we braved it very well and returned to the Bull & Mouth about ½ past 8 where we supped and I left them about ½ past 9 and agreed to meet them on Sunday morning at 7 o'clock - came home very weary, smoked a pipe, drank a glass of stout and retired to rest. Rose about 4 this morning, half dress'd, smoked a pipe then set to earnestly to write a letter to my dear Friend Forbes Dobb[54] which I did under emotions peculiarly painful, for he had not sent me a line by Edward Hoyle whom he had seen but a short time previous, I scarcely know what by feelings were, how can it be accounted for? what have I done? do I deserve to be thus slighted? and by one for whom and his family I have been very much persecuted. This Satisfaction is mine. I know I do not deserve it. Well! but I have asked him and he will doubtless explain the cause - met Edward Hoyle at the Swan Pier I believe it is called just above London Bridge a little past 8 A M and went on board the 'Hardy' steamer with him which was engaged to take the passengers down to Gravesend where the British Queen was lying, the morning was wet and very unfavorable; went on the 'Queen' about ¼ to 11 A M and was there more surprised at the achieve-ments of human skill than I had ever been before I had nothing like a just perception of her magnitude, compactness and splendour - partook of some biscuit and cheese and a bottle of Dublin Stout, and then partially gratified my curiosity that then enabled me to say that not only had I seen the present wonder of the scientific and mechanical world, but that I had eaten and drank there:— staid on board about an hour saw Edward snugly settled for his long journey, having seen his luggage all right, secured his berth also that of his Sister, and was very happy to see them appear comfortable and composed in the varied scenes by which they were surrounded. Some countenances beaming with hope and eyes lit by joy in the anticipation of another sight of their Transatlantic homes: some wore a sullen gloom looked borne down with grief and while others sobbed aloud, lovely eyes suffused in tears, would occasionally steal a melancholy glance at the endearing beacons, which point to scenes of early days, and conjure up a host of past events, commencing with the tricks of childhood and the Parents fond embraces with all the varied scenes Times hand has wrought, even to the painful hour that tolls the last Farewell to all once held so dear, but now thought doubly so! may not all the gazings of the sprightly few can quell one throb or quench one burning tear - Oh! for the power to moralise on such events as these tis here we see the workings strong of nature when Friends of dearest ties and nearest sympathies are brought to take a long a last fond look and trust unto the merciless waves. This done I saw the noble mistress of the sea steer out of Gravesend at 12 o'clock (noon) precisely: She got under weigh a little before but had to go up the river before she could turn round so huge were her dimensions - the 'Hardy' accompanied her up but looked only like a galley compared to her; Farewell said many a voice and in my inmost soul I wished the same to everyone on Board - went to the 'Popes' Head' public house, drank a pint of ale (charged 5d) 4d of gin smoked a pipe of Tobacco; and ret'd. by the first Boat at 3 o'clock to London which we reached at ½ past 5 - saw a steam boat on fire off Gravesend burning most terrifically, all efforts to check the devouring element during our observation appeared useless but I have learned this evening that she was afterwards scuttled and sunk [55] - Took tea at home, and went to bed as soon as night put on her dark attire, being much fatigued before, but now am more by writing out this dull account of one long days' adventure.

Monday September 2 - 1839 Rose about 7 felt very much refreshed having rested well, sent a note to Mr. Stringfellow [56] at Providence House [57] - but he was out and I did not receive an answer - dined as usual at one look'd at the paper nothing important in it - weighed off 25lbs of Beaver and 50lbs of Nutria sides opened a pack from home which I find has been in since Saturday there is one body too many in it David wishes me to send him a receipt to make proofing [58] the bodies are good - went to Mr. Coopers [59] with 1 lb of Beaver we had borrowed of them, and brought 1 bag of Nutria to compare with ours; in the Evening a Bag of Red wool came in from Borradaile & Co's did not weigh it intend to do that in the morning when I can see better down stairs - sent for 1 Pot of Porter J.I. [60] and myself drank it, I smoked a pipe read a little in an old Sheffield Iris - then wrote this paragraph - weather very wet and cold. sent a box of hats home. P.S. Received a new coat & Waistcoat in the parcel from home, they write all well. Thank God. current expenses 7s 9d.

Tuesday September 3rd Rose about 7 A M proceeded to business after breakfast no one at work but the dyer & One tipper off until about ½ past 10 when the finishers commenced, trade awfully bad the money market depressed and deplorable accounts from the manufacturing districts the rate of Discount in London upon Tradesmens Bills being from 15 to 30 Per Cent, says the Morning Chronicle - things are really awful Mr Scott Mr Irwin & Mr Rittson [61] all started their regular journeys on Saturday last but we have not yet received an order - Looked over some Nutria when Mr. I bought of Paynes' Brothers found it equal to Coopers' lot, at least I thought so, there were 3 oz short weight which they sent up afterwards - After business hours went in company with J. In to see M Stringfellow and his friends at Providence House. Falcon St. staid until ½ past 10 then came thro' Bartholomew Fair had one pint of ale at Peter Crawleys and one glass of Brandy & water at Ludgate Hill got home rather past midnight. Weather showery current expenses 10s having paid for the weeks' before dinners.

Wedensday September 4 Rose about ½ past 8 A M when the Post came - anticipated some trade but was most woefully disappointed which cast a gloom over me which the day has not dispelled. Mr R is in Hull & has not sent an order: What will be next? the account of the money market *rather* more favorable not much - sent off a hat to Dronfield for John Hydes - but was rather too late for the Coach and with it a letter to my Parents and returned one body which we had received above the number Invoiced I was still very gloomy smoked a pipe at dusk ate a little supper wrote these observations and am now preparing to retire to rest in the hope that next day may present better appearances of trade - weather very fine. Current expenses 1s 1½d. PS mentioned Jim[62] coming to London in my letter home.

Thursday September 5 1839   Rose about ½ past 5 A M and went in company with John Irwin to Billingsgate Market - bought some Fresh Herrings 1s per Dozen Mr Stringfellow call'd after breakfast accompanied him & his friends to London Bridge; then went to Fullers[63] bought two Low. Cro. Hoods for Ritsons order, came home and dined; little trade from Mr Scott Mr Stringfellow & friends called and took tea with us preparatory to us visiting the 'Surrey Zoo-logical Garden'[64] were joined after tea by a Gent. who is a hatter from Halifax Nova Scotia, and who had been purchasing hats in London he looked at some of our goods and expressed himself pleased with them and kindly promised to send to us when he wanted more goods from London his name is Robinson went to the Gardens was very much delighted by the spendid display of fireworks consequent upon the Eruption which is Said to imitate that of Mount Hecla and the eruption itself far surpassed my conception of it, altho I had seen the artificial mountain on a former occasion (but not an eruption) and reflects the highest credit on the Artists:— was very wet on our return call'd in at the Half Moon Boro'[65] for shelter went from thence to Providence House where I supped and took sundry glasses of wine with Mr. Ritson and Mr. Stringfellow after the rest of the party had retured to rest. came home and went to bed about ½ past 11 P M - current expenses 2s 6d. Weather very wet in the evening day changeable.

Friday September 6th   Rose at 8 A M waited eagerly for Post time not a single order came was half melancholy during the day by reflecting so much on the aspect of affairs and the prospects of the people went to the Brown Bear at night had half a pint of ale then came home ½ past nine prepared for bed full of hopes & fears about trade etc

Saturday September 7 1839   Rose at ½ past 7 - Post came to Samuda[66] next door and did not call here - was completely horror stricken drunk a cup of coffee, eat I could not was however very agreeably relieved from that unpleasant state about ½ past 9 when another Postman came and brought some very satis-factory letters from Mr Irwin & Mr Scott and one for 5 Doz I think from Lumsden & Com. of Tralee J. I. & myself set to work earnestly and look'd out every order, but one from Scott of Wakefield who wants them cutting very short - work'd very hard and very cheerfully all day then went to Boro' Market at night J. I. bought 2 cauliflowers 2d each had ½ pint of beer each at the Harrow then started off home. I went to smoke a pipe with the toll keeper at the Bridge [67] and got to bed about ½ past 11 P M written the morning following.

Sunday September 8/39   Rose at 7 A M wash'd looked over the paper smoked etc. till breakfast was ready after breakfast commenced getting a great quantity of corks out of a bottle which occupied my time till dinner was ready and an hour afterwards however I succeeded and so was satisfied for my impression is, if a man earnestly commences a thing, however trivial it may be he ought not to give up while there is any possibility of succeeding, for if he does he thereby loses hold of those habits of settled perseverance, which are so necessary to promote his welfare went in the afternoon with J. I. to Chelsea by a steamer saw nothing to note refreshed about 1 mile farther up with 2 pts of ale and then returned to London by a steamer where we arrived at 8 P M the wind was very high over part of the time on our going up to Chelsea calmer as we returned had 1 Glass of ale each at the Half Moon Boro' and 1½ dozen of Oysters in Union St for which we paid the exhorbitant charge of 13d - walked leisurely home, gave the mare her mash - I then wrote the present paragraph and now intend to smoke a pipe over a pint of Porter have a chat and retire to rest, 'tis now 10 o'clock.

Monday September 8/39   Rose about 8 A M nothing particular to note during the day - went to Astleys [68] in the Evening ½ price noticed the performances with considerable interest and was really surprised at the tractability of a huge Elephant which amongst other tricks lifted his keeper above the ground with his trunk, placed him snugly on his tusks and carried him around the arena and from thence off the stage, the horsemanship was truly astonishing (one man I believe a German) performed many feats, he rode at full speed and threw up and catched 4 balls for some time, then 2 balls & 2 cups all of which he threw up occasionally catching the cups & then the balls in them - was also much pleased with a Mr. Sheppard in the character of 'Timour the Tartar' this appears to me a most arduous task for amongst many other feats he rides on the near [*Blank*] of the horse as if he was fastened thereto his legs coming almost to the ground the horse being without any harness whatever not so much as a bridle, he then appears to fall off and remounts, lying with his back across the horses' back his head on one side and feet on the other the performance was altogether very interesting and was another proof to me of the remarkable power and ingenuity of man when especially directed to any particular object - came away between 11 - 12 P M called at a house on my way home and saw a person in a masquarade dress in the character of a *milestone* '4 miles from London' being printed on, came home from thence to bed.

Tuesday September 10 1839   Rose at 8 A M pursued my business through the day and at night retired at 10 o'clock - weather very fine - News rather more encouraging in a commercial point of view.

Wedensday September 11   Rose at 6 A M rather foggy in the early part of the morning went thro' my usual routine of business - sent off a pack to Rugeley - did not like some of Higgitts' bodies which I looked over. Sent one off to Dronfield also per Pickfords and also some washing with them, promised to write tomorrow with a small pack per Coach which I now must do, worked hard all the day - Weather *very* fine & *very* hot after the morning part.

Thursday September 12   Rose about 6 A M pursued my usual calling sent a small pack and in it a letter to my Father & a long ditto to David walked out 1 hour in the Evening - had a pint of beer went to bed at ½ past 10 P M. Weather very fine.

Friday September 13 1839   Rose at 4 A M under the impression that some one was in the premises, look over the different rooms but found all quite safe and that my impression was the produce of a confused mind having awoke very suddenly out of a dream - staid up till daylight let in the Porters then laid down and slept until 8 o'clock went the usual round of business in the course of the day had some very serious talk with J. I. upon the foolish way we spent some of our leisure time and some of our money by what was said betwixt us I was not only convinced of the folly of it but was absolutely determined to alter the practice and following up that conviction I purpose to commence reading, not casually but systematically and to begin this night with 'Watts Logic'[69] and read at the rate of 20 pages per day as near as the division of the subject will allow provided my health will permit me, for however pressing business may be which shall not on any Account be neglected I intend to accomplish the *task* of reading the work through in the space of 16 days for the first time and then to read it through a second time more closeley and make notes, or rather to lay down such other plan as may afterwards seem most likely to accomplish my object that object being 'A right use of Reason' - so here goes for the work and if I cannot subdue myself so much as to enable me to effect it, I must be unworthy of the name of man, of the remembrance of many surmounted difficulties with which I have before contended and also of those powers which a Kind Providence has bestowed upon me. *'Diligentia omnia vincit* 8 o'clock P M

Saturday September 14/39   Rose at 8 having been uneasy during the night which I attributed to eating pork to dinner it not being well cooked, went the normal round of duty, went to Boro' Market in the Evening with J. I. we bought a small haddock and some potatoes for Sunday dinner, had 3 pints of Beer at the Harrow then came home, I afterwards read my apportioned quantity of 'Watt's

Logic', smoked a pipe and am now ready to retire to rest. Trade very dull - Weather very wet and rather windy as predicted by Murphy [70] ½ past 12.

Sunday September 15 1839   Rose about ½ past 8 A M worked in the Dyehouse then bathed in one of the becks which had been prepared on the Saturday Evening read until near Dinner time had a walk on the Bankside came home and dined on a little Haddock we had bought the previous Evening cost 5s walked out again over London Bridge etc. until Tea time after tea went with J. I. to a Chapel at the bottom of Union Street heard a good discourse from the Gospel of St. John 'The Wind bloweth where it listeth etc etc' the principal of elucidation of the Text was to them that there are many things in nature as well as revelation which cannot be fully comprehended but that their effects are so visible we cannot refuse to believe them - came home, had a glass of gin & water read my quantum of Watts Logic smoked a pipe and am now ready to retire to rest. Weather wet & cold - feel very happy & composed on the manner we have spent the day having had only 1 pint of beer betwixt us 11 P M.

Monday September 16 1839   Rose at ½ past 7 A M was informed by a card found inside the door of Mr Irwins arrival he came up to the premises about ½ past 10. gave an alarming account of the state of trade in the districts he had travelled. he brought very few orders - found he had not seen any of our people in Sheffield but had sent them word of his coming through Dronfield was very sorry on that account for I much wished him to see some of them respecting brother James coming to London: we looked out in the course of the day the chief part of his orders. was very unhappy in the afternoon, caused chiefly by reflecting too much on the state of trade and contemplating the gloomy prospects of the country during the approaching season, ate nothing at 7 P M felt rather more cheerful had a pipe of tobacco and 1 pint of beer, took a little supper and afterwards read 28 pages of 'Watts Logic' now feel weary and am on the point of retiring with the hope that my evenings improvement will be a little set off for the cares of the day - What can the government of a great country like this be doing to allow so many of its industrious and enterprising merchants and tradesmen to be inevitably ruined and its laborious and skilful mechanics and artisans plunged into the most grievous distress. - When will governors become just? the people require only to live by their labor but *this* is denied them and that heavy curse first denounced of direst fallen man' would now by millions of my fellow countrymen be deemed a blessing - Weather very showery: — trade *very* bad - prospect *very* gloomy - St. Pauls' clock has just announced the time to be 11 P M. -

Tuesday September 17/39   Rose about ½ past 8 A M having passed rather a restless night, breakfasted and proceeded to business: — men all at work. Received a pack from home in the Evening open'd it, but found not a word to myself, save a note from my sister Harriatt [71] along with some clean linens - much disappointed but however I will write tomorrow if all be well and send a few fine odd bodies which we are in want of. - have felt very gloomy and dejected a great part of the day, have no positive cause for it, and really it must be a folly for me to trouble my mind about the state of trade etc when all my sorrow will not alter it in the least. Weather very wet, trade very dull - now going to bed having completed my daily reading 12 o'clock - News today of Don Carlos quitting Spain and taking refuge in France. which is likely to terminate the civil war in Spain.[72]

Wedensday September 18/39   Rose at 8 A M followed my business closely through the day - in the course of which I opened a pack from home and found a letter from my Father, wherein they dissented from my plan of James coming to London for this I was very sorry to see how people who have seen little of the world do confine their ideas, centralise their affections and blight many cheering prospects wrote them again for a positive answer sent off the letter with a pack of 3 Dozen odd fine bodies and the balance of their Account £40 18 sent it off per 'Rapid Coach' Castle and Falcon - had a walk as far as Temple Bar in the Evening - felt unwell from a headache purchased some medicine in Blackfriars Rd. came home about ½ past 10 P M read my stinted quantity of 'Watts' now intend to smoke a pipe, take a Calomel [73] Pill and go to bed - Weather very fine in the morning. - rather wet a time or two during the course of the day:— very unfavourable for the late harvest [*Crossed through:* Heard -(& not correct 'Charles the 12th 'having won Major Yarburghs) of Bloomsbury winning the St Leger and tho' not pecuniarily interested was much pleased because of the injustice practised upon his owner Mr Ridsdale)]

Thursday September 19/39   Rose at ½ past 6 A M nothing particular occurred throughout the day - was very unwell the greatest part of it. owing to the effects of my medicine - noticed at dinner time the improper conduct of Mr. Slyfield [74]   he having taken the paper and not reading aloud. I kindly requested him to read the 'City Article' and sat ¼ of an hour thinking he would look at it in awhile, he however continued reading to himself and *deigned not* to answer me or to comply with my request or to give up the paper but sat as if he were the only person who had a right to know any of its contents, and also as if he were a being superior to us - Here was a subject for my philosophy, I was at first rather indignant for my unvarying practice is to treat all people with civility and I therefore claim civility from others but afterwards thought my being offended might answer some purpose of the party and therefore determined to let it pass away, as if unnoticed, I record this to show the progress of that contemptible spirit if it should manifest itself on any other occasion - Weather very unsettled, read my usual quantity, and retired quite fatigued.

56

Friday September 20   Rose at 7 A M felt much better than I had done the two previous days went thro' my business very cheerfully - was only too sorry there was so little to do, cleared up every order save one stout hat, this is truly alarming for the winter prospects I don't know what will become of tradesmen unless things alter very much and that soon. - came into the sitting room and read for an hour (or so) then went to a house in the Street and had 1 pint of beer came home a little before 10 and am writing the present paragraph.

Weather remarkably fine considering how wet and uncertain it had been for some days past - until about 9 P M when it commenced raining heavily. I am really alarmed for the consequences our staple and foreign trades being already so much depressed and am afraid the unfavorable harvest weather will seriously affect our domestic and home trade - Mr Irwin has cautioned me against stocking many ruffed hats either gray, black or finished but says 100 or 150 Dozen bodies wont harm because we have the materials all in stock. 11 o'clock.

Saturday September 21   Rose about ½ past 7 had very little to do in the course of the day - reckoned at 6 P M went to market bought some potatoes for Sunday - also some nuts - the eating of which made me quite sick and ill - went to bed about 12 rather easier Mr Ritson having written for 6 or 7 Dozen things still very flat, weather wet and all things partaking of the gloom P.S. did not read my stated quantity.

Sunday September 22   Rose at 9 A M having passed a very restless night, breakfasted and then washed in the Dyers beck, after dinner rode up to Paddington to make inquiries after Charles Turner made all the inquiry I could, but could not hear any thing of him, came home had tea read until near 10 o'clock the weather had been very wet 'till about 9 after which it cleared up and I walked up and down the road till 11 o'clock very fine & moonlight, discovered some very disagreeable company upon me in the morning how I came by them I cannot tell (*lice*) have applied a remedy but have been very uneasy concerning them all day - they have not made much progress and I hope to arrest them shortly - this is a strange thing to record but it is done to enable me to ascertain the mode I came by them, and so be prepared to avoid a recurrence, for I am sure no one could be more particular in washing and changing their linen - now for bed ½ past 11.

Monday September 23   Rose ½ past 7 received a very kind letter from my Father wherein he stated his willingness for James to come to London, and left it for me to agree with Mr Irwin, at this I was very glad altho aware of the grief it will cause my mother it appears to me desirable to teach James his trade fully that he may be enabled to locate in some populous district and so benefit both himself and the family for seeing that David is married and settled at Dronfield he will be quite sufficient to manage the business there and were James to stay there also a division of interests might be caused by some unforeseen event therefore do I think it will be best for each of us to have a different interest so united that they may be productive of the greatest possible interest for the whole. How far my plan may succeed God only knows, but he knows also the purity of my motives and my humble prayer to him is that he will assist me to carry them out so far as they are agreeable to his will. - Went in the Evening to a low public house, solely for the purpose of observing a company which had collected there for the purpose of raffling off two birds which belonged to one of our late Dyers who is out of work, there was a lesson for the opposers of education, men and women chiefly Irish whose appearance bespoke almost destitution drinking, dancing and bawling, wasting their time so frivolously and spending their money so lavishly that clearly shewed they had no just opinion of its value, nor any prospective view of their future wants nay, nor any of their present absolute wants: staid about an hour, came away quite satisfied with the results of my curiosity for I had not any just conception before of the manner these poor creatures (whose general appearances indicated wretchedness) squandered away their means - did not read much to night but if all be well I intend to bring up the arrears tomorrow 12 o'clock.

Tuesday September 24   Rose at 8 A M proceeded to my usual duties - commenced reading at 7 P M and continued until ½ past 9 made up for the last nights neglect and am now going to bed nearly 10 P M - weather very unsettled, accounts of the harvest in different parts of the country very bad.

Wedensday September 25/39   Rose at 6 A M look over and gave out work was very busy until 10 A M when I went to the West India Docks to pick some Logwood [75]   (price Eleven Pounds per Ton) went over the docks saw many vessels discharging their cargoes principally consisting of Sugar, Rum & Woods - this was the first time I had ever had so good an opportunity of observing the extensive accomodation which is made for our Commerce I could not dare even to guess at the vast number of Hogsheads of Sugar, Punchions of Rum, Pipes of Wine and Iron vessels (in the form of Solid Quadrants) filled with Cocoa nut oil, which I saw there, beside the immense stacks of Wood chiefly mahogany and Dye Woods some of the logs of Mahogany were 6 tons weight, the stock of Logwood was said to be very small - there were hundred of men at work - many scores of coopers repairing Sugar Hogsheads etc which had been damaged in the carriage and unloading - the size of the premises I have no just conception of, they are so immense, there was one room alone full of Rum Puncheons, which cannot be less than one acre in extent, and cellaring under it of equal size; the Warehouses which are all roofed with copper are very extensive said to be the most so of any in London and therefore I presume the most extensive in the world:— here I could not but reflect on what the skill and enterprise of man had accomplished, the vast amount of labour - created capital which was presented

58

to my eye at one view in the form of Premises, Vessels and Goods all of which must be a fraction compared to the Property which annually nay daily is there Imported and Exported - and then conclude that this, with all that my conceptions could add to it in the form of commerce daily carried on in the other docks in the Port of London - and the different Ports of the Kingdom - had grown to its present importance despite the restrictions which had been imposed upon it by a lazy band of Aristocratic Legislators, who have neither the skill nor the enterprise to engage in such vast undertakings, the conducting of which furnish us with all the valuable productions of other counties in exchange for the various commodities of this country: — yet with all that has been done in spite of them, I am grieved to know that our surplus commodities which are at this time superabundant cannot be allowed to be given in exchange for the superabundance of food in other countries, while our artisans are famished for want of food which can only be supplied to them by the medium of labor, and other nations are equally deprived of our goods because they have nothing to give in Exchange for them but food - their food is consequently wasted and themselves deprived of many necessary adjuncts of civilisation while our goods are lying on the hands of our Merchants and Manufacturers our workmen wanting employment, consequently famishing: — this is the lot of many thousands of industrious men at the present day, and all to serve the purposes of the Landowning Lawmakers, who appear determined at every risk and at the sacrifice of every human feeling to continue their odious system, even though it should ultimately destroy the very means of supporting themselves in their exalted and unnatural stations - which means certainly are (abstractedly considered) the trade and commerce of the Kingdom. Oh! that the next time they meet in the capacity of Legislators they may see the evil of their past proceedings and amend it by just and salutary laws, which shall be the means of enabling the industrious to live by their industry, - the indefatigable tradesman to be justly remunerated for his toil and harrassing duties and the enterprising merchant to be well rewarded for his spirited exertions as the means of causing a just interchange of commodity between man and man, nation and nation. I have carried these observations to a great length, but perhaps they will do to refer to at another period, for my opinions are that with the present state of the money market there being only between 2 & 3 millions in the 'Bank of England' the bad state of trade and the very unfavourable weather for the harvest, that it will be next to impossible to prevent a change in the 'Corn Laws' the next session of Parliament. - Rained very fast at 6 A M was fine and warm during the day then commenced raining again about 9 P M -

Underwrote an Invoice to Mr Booth Sheffield and sent a letter to James Turner - went out for 10 minutes then came home opened a bottle of Porter and wrote this Account of the days' transactions - forgot to say we were much hindered at the Docks having had to wait nearly an hour for a pass etc. (received a note from J. Jarvis of Brampton Moor).[76] now ½ past 11, & ready for bed.

Thursday September 26   Rose a little before 8 A M felt rather fatigued from the effects of the previous days' labor, went in the Evening to Ivyleafe, Regent Street[77] to inquire after a situation as an apprentice for the young man whom J. Jervis recommended to me, saw Mr Rawle the foreman who was very civil but said he could not do anything with the young man - walk'd smartly back - brought the young man home with me for supper - went out and had a glass of beer over the way and 1 pint at the Harrow came home and am ready for bed ½ past 12. - weather very fine.

Friday September 27   Rose at ¼ past 8 A M - in the course of the day sent a pack off to Dronfield per Pickfords on Railway consisting of 18 Dozen wool bodies 6 dozen nappings, 8 dozen Jerries and nappings and 6 dozen E1 bodies enclosed 3 Day shirts 1 night do 1 singlet & 1 pr of stockings to be washed - supped on a Roasted Onion, read and am now ready for bed - weather very fine and hot. - 10 o'clock P M

Saturday September 28   Rose ½ past 6 A M received 66lb of Nutria sides into stock from Mr. Bates' price 24s weighed napping for 12 doz. wools which I intended to have sent by coach for the bodies which were sent by Railway on Friday also 4 dozen Jerries. Ask'd Mr. I. about sending for Brother James to come up but received no positive answer therefore deferred sending the pack until Monday that I might write them more fully than the then present time allowed me to do. - In the Evening I drew Ten Pounds on account of my Salary and fulfilled a promise which I had made to J. I. - went with him over the water, we then called in at the Harrow and had each 4d of gin & water. came home at ½ past 11 P M and retired to rest at 12. - Weather fine.

Sunday September 29   Rose at 7 A M cleaned & dressed before breakfast. The morning was remarkably fine - walked out after breakfast called on John Bryson[78] came home and dined on bread & cheese. J. I. and myself walked out after dinner when wet. Met with a young person with whom I went to Greenwich in a steamer, walked out in the park there - took tea and returned by Railway - about 7 o'clock called at Deverell St.[79] Staid there until past 10 o'clock and walked home not very well pleased with what had transpired there got home ¼ to 11 - and am now ready for bed - The finest day of the summer.

Monday September 30   Rose at 7 A M - gave the Finishers work out - wrote a letter to Jervis and one to my Parents which I enclosed in the pack that was prepared on Saturday but sent off this day by Coach 'Rapid' Went to the Anniversary Dinner of the 'St Olaves' Lodge[80] held at the Brown Bear Bridge Road at 5 P M - spent a very pleasant evening - and came home at ½ past 11 -

have not time to write much, feel ready for bed - another very fine day. -

Tuesday October 1st 1839   Rose ½ past 8 A M - weigh'd out 1 doz 40 low. cro. for Tate of Liverpool. nothing else particular another fine day -

Wedensday October 2   Rose at ½ past 6 A M - went the usual round of duty. Mr Cooper came up about noon to borrow 3 lbs of White wooms Beaver which I lent to him, - in the afternoon had some unpleasant words with Slyfield concerning his officiousness in putting up a letter box - because we having been accustomed to receive the letters I was of opinion that the alteration implied a want of confidence, which I stated to him and asked if there were any cause for it and whether it was Mr Irwins' order - he told me it was not, but *he* considered 'it was *not proper* for the letters to go up stairs' - Whereupon I said if it were not proper, it was improper and wished to know why it was improper as no letter had been opened nor had there been the least delay - for I had invariably given them into his hands as soon as he arrived in the mornings - expressed my intention of naming it to T. I. - feeling as I do convinced that it is an instance of a systematic tho' quiet persecution which has been for some time practised towards J. I. & myself in the forms of slighting and doubting - here many things seem to my memory which produce great uneasiness - I have left a peaceful and happy home, given up a dear circle of acquaintance, and foregone the views I had of commencing a business of my own to remain like a watch dog on an almost homeless (as far as the Society of home goes) premises discharging my duties assiduously & faithfully to the best of my ability, and after all to be scorned or doubted by a puppy scarcely out of his teens? if so I am off from London the first time my engagement will permit me for it ill accords with my feelings whose mottoe it is to pay due respect to all men, to be subjected to any such behaviour let it come from whom it may - I thank God that I have the means to help myself to a greater degree of happiness even by manual labour so long as he preserves my strength, than can ever result from such treatment as I am at present subject to. - Who? before this upstart ever refused to answer a civil question from me? or if answered done with the greatest contumely - no one, for I never deserved it and until I do - I will not submit to it. - of this I have had many instances and many other tokens of disrespect which are not worth recording:— for true philosphy should teach me not to be annoyed by such proceedings but a regard to my own character compels me to notice them. Enough at present - smoked a pipe in the evening & drank 1 pint of beer - the weather which had been fine during the day turned out rainy in the Evening - read & wrote until 11 P M and am now ready for bed with almost a wish but that would be unmanly that I was on my Fathers' Hearth listening to the sage advice of my dear Parents, or else enjoying repose in my old couch.

Thursday October 3   Rose about 7 proceeded to business after breakfast

Mr I. came up to town - mentioned the affair of the Letter Box to him - he said he could not think it was intended to cast any imputation upon our characters tho' he appeared very cautious in speaking about it and said he would see to it: — in the Evening William Booth & a Mr. Booth Grocer from Sheffield came in they smoked a pipe with us and we afterwards had a glass of ale at the Half Moon in the Boro W.B. gave an order for a Hat for self and 3 Fancies for his children for which he paid me 2 £1 [i.e. £2?] - I paid the cash into Mr. Slyfield's hands - saw no more of Mr. I this day - came home at ½ past 10 P M and am ready for bed - weather very fine trade rather more lively - Mr. S - returned this day from his Western Journey.

Friday October 4   Went to business soon after I arose 7 A M and nearly worked myself out before tea-time was skulking in the packing room when Mr I came to me and asked me to go to his house and take a Beefstake with him at ½ past 8 P M he also invited J. I. and J S who were standing in the room left the premises at 8 P M with J I and we walked down and spent a very pleasant Evening - the company consisted of a Mr. Earle a Mr. Pearce and Mr Barr - besides Messes J. I. J S - H S - and myself came away about ½ past 11 P M and came direct home - a fine day but came on wet in the Evening very fine at midnight

Saturday October 5   Rose a little before 9 - very unwell having a severe pain in my back which I attributed to having slept with the bedroom window wide open on Thursday night - had a dye of hats came up in the morning which did not please me they were too light in colour reckoned a little before 7 P M and afterwards read the paper & smoked a pipe - received and entered 10s on account from [Blank] then sold 7 old hats to Yarwood for 11s went with J.I. to Market bought 1 pair of fine soles for 8d - 2 fresh Herrings for 1½ and 3 lbs of Potatoes for 3d - called at Wheelers had 1 pint of beer each - then came home at 11 P M and am now ready for bed - received a box from home with 10 doz ruffs - weather very fine -

Sunday October 6   Rose at ½ past 7 - lighted the fire & cleaned up the hearth - William Booth came to breakfast after which he & myself had a walk before dinner - about ½ past 2 he, Mr I & myself walked up to St James Park thro' there and Hyde Park to the top of the water, over the bridge of the Serpentime & back again on the top side of the Park to Oxford Street refreshed with a Pint of Ale & a biscuit each in Oxford Street then walked to T Springs' had 2 pints of ale there amongst us came home at ½ past 9 smoked a pipe each after supper & am now ready for bed - I think this has been the finest day of the year

Monday October 7   Rose at ¼ past 6 A M in the course of business opened a pack from home & one from Rugely, entered them duly and sent the Invoices to the Counting House. Mr. Scott staid a little later in the Evening smoked a pipe and had a very comfortable chat with us, was much pleased with this, as it appears to me to be quite proper for fellow servants to converse freely, when a release from business permits it for by those means each becomes better acquainted with the nature of the trade and thereby knows which is the most likely way to serve the different parties; and many other little circumstances which are proper to be known - indeed altogether have spent an agreeable evening - and am now ready for bed a little before 10 P M - a very fine day

Tuesday October 8   Rose ½ past 6 A M, pursued my business throughout the day and in the evening went to the Prince & Princess Gravel Lane to see Thos. Hunt who had sent a note to me had 2 pints of beer with him gave him 2s and came away about 9 P M - fell in with Mr Embleton [81] who requested me to tell Mr. Irwin to come over to his house if he should be in Town in the morning - walked as far as the Elephant & Castle looking at the shops - and as it were wasting my time as frivolously as I could came home a little before 11 P M - Very fine day.

Wedensday October 9   Rose at 7 A M one of the most delightful mornings I ever noticed in London, it continued so until ½ past 10 A M when there came on a very smart shower - had some foolish work in the Afternoon amongst the women,[82]   which appeared to me very ridiculous, for I have long seen if a man will trouble himself with the paltry tales and disputes of women he will always be in trouble, Mr T. Irwin spoke rather sharply upon the subject the first time he has used anything like a harsh expression to me indeed I can scarcely characterize it as harshness as he might probably have had some improper stories instilled in to his Ear, and thought that mode expression the most likely to obtain a thorough knowledge of the foolish case - but that did not answer upon me - he says he will now fully investigate the matter tomorrow I *wish* he may but cannot suppress a smile at some of the statements which have been made - sent off a pack to Rugely and enclosed 5 bodies to be replaced we had an order for 10½ dozen from Leech & Robinson, Oxford who called, another very fine day - smoked a pipe in the Evening with Mr S & J.I. & Wm Booth called in about ½ past 9 - now ready for bed ½ past 11 P M.

Thursday October 10 39   Rose at 8 A M was very much pleased to hear of another good business letter from Mr Rittson from Dublin went to work very cheerfully - took out a good many of the hats gave out others to be finished and to the best of my judgment facilitated the business was not very well pleased in the Evening to see that not any of them had been given out to round - am really [*Blank*] to see how some people let very little matters throw them off their balance of temper. - smoked a pipe with Mr S & J.I. and afterwards went to Wheelers - where my friends took 1 glass each of Gin & Water & myself 1 pint of ale, very fine day -

Friday October 11   Rose at 7 A M in the course of the day shopped a maker of the name of T. Harrison from Denton - staid up until 12 Midnight with the Dyer who was working to get a Dye of Fine hats out on the Saturday - a very fine day and the prospects rather better - ½ past 12.

Saturday October 12/39   Rose about 7 - was very busy all day with one thing & another weigh'd the tare of a Pod of Verdigris from Borrodaile & Cos which was rather under ¾lb, had 1 lb. tare allowed so that was all right: also weighed out a mixing of proofing viz 40 lb Shellac 10 lb Sandrick 3 lb Mastick - 4 Gal spirits wine 4 lb of Frn [*Frankincense*], 5 Rosin 2 gal Turps, - went to market at ½ past 9 P M bought fish & potato for Sundays Dinner had 2 - 4d of Gin & water each came home smoked a pipe drank 1 bottle of Porter each and conversed until ½ past 2 Sunday morning - much rain in the course of the Friday night but this day Saturday was very warm & fine. received 10s of [*Blank*]

Sunday October 13/39   Rose about 10 A M and was very much afflicted with the head-ache, had a cup of tea and laid down again got a little more sleep after which, was somewhat better when I awoke there was a very rapid discharge of mucous appeared to come out of my head down what I suppose is called the frontal cynus, this relieved me considerably - believe it to be the effect of cold which I had got on Friday night & Saturday - walked out after dinner with J.I. & Wm Booth called at Booths' lodgings I doubt he is not in a good way - the situation he has chosen and the company he keeps are not likely to improve him - this is my opinion - called at Mr Deacons and Mr. Jones' got home about 7 P M much better - weather very fine -

Monday October 14   Nothing particular occurred the day very fine received a pack of bodies from home and some clothes.

Tuesday 15   Weighed out in the course of the day 24 doz Jerries - a young man came to be apprenticed - I did not know what to put him to, as Mr. Irwin had not said anything about him - so told him to come again tomorrow - was much annoyed by the conduct of Mr Wouldbe I called repeatedly for Martin, he has sent him out but had not the civility to say so, altho' it is customary in the house to say so when another party calls - went to my room and felt very uneasy at the thought of being so grossly insulted by such a puppy more especially when my memory pointed out the place I had occupied in society at home which was voluntarily abandoned by me to come to London, yet at Mr. I's urgent request, I almost determined the moment my agreement was fulfilled to leave London and find an occupation more congenial to my feelings - but I must think about it, perhaps that would suit the party.

Wedensday October 16   Rose at ½ past 6 - Mr. Irwin came up and said he had forgot to mention the young man Stephens - he told me to send the Jerries to

Mr. Coopers' at Ashton to be made - Mr. Dunean dined with us on boiled beef & peas pudding - in the Afternoon Mr. Irwin invited me to a glass of Brandy & Water with himself & Mr. Dn which I took & 3 cigars he gave to me, had a short walk in the Evening with J.I. - called at H's had 1 pint each of half & half came home & am ready for bed ½ past 10 P M - frosty.

Thursday October 17 Rose at ½ past 7 - after breakfast two of the Makers came to me to say that part of one mans Home's napping was missing. I invest-igated the matter very closely but could not ascertain who was the thief - had a glass of Gin & Water after dinner with Mr Scott who was just going his Midland Journey - took stock of Finished hats in the Evening - including returns - they amounted to about 45 dozen (all sorts) smoked a pipe and am now ready to read a little & go to bed 9 P M Fine day rather frosty.

Friday October 18/39 Rose ½ past 6 - received a pack of 3 doz B1 from home - and with them letter from David wherein he told me that a New fair was to be held this day at Dronfield,[83] and that there was a good prospect of success for it:— was very much pleased at this, as it is a proof of there being some public spirit in the place to undertake the affair and anything tending to improve my native village is highly gratifying to me - for I still revere it and very many of its inhabitants - sent a pack of 24 doz D1 to be made to Mr Coopers' Ashton and enclosed 2£ 5s to S. Howarth for making 6 doz Silk Shells and 2 Bx bodies sent short before [*Blank*] a youth committed suicide by leaping off the Monument this Evening[84] have not heard particulars a very fine day - business gloomy - had a bottle of porter, and am ready for bed. 10 P M

Sat October 19 Rose about 7 A M - read orders from Mr. Irwin not to give any more work to a young man of the name of Stephens who came on trial as an Apprentice, he also told me to go or send to Borrodaile & Co on Monday morning for some Cheek Beaver; reckoned about 7 after which J.I. and myself walked as far as Cockertons' in the Minories - had 1 pint of ale each, called at Wheelers and had each another came home a little past 11 P M - received 10s of [*Blank*] a very fine day.

Sunday October 20 The bell was rung before I rose this morning, and on my looking out saw a young woman with a basket in her hand - partly dressed and opened the door she inquired for W. H. Latham[85] Silk Finisher and told me she was his wife and had just come up from Hull by a steamer in search of him - that she had not seen him for 12 months and that she had heard he had got married again in London - I invited her in to give me an opportunity of finding out his residence for her. Jno. Irwin knew the place, but after a little consideration we thought it best to send for him, and Mayes went to his house in Gunpowder Alley Shoe Lane where he found him and induced by a plausible story to come with him not mentioning the woman to him - he first denied having any wife but the one he was now living with but upon being introduced to the Stranger he said 'she was his wife but he should not own her' and added that he was married to the woman he lived with and was quite regardless of the consequences; some little altercation ensued between them but he persisted in saying he would prefer transportation to living with his first and lawful wife:— she added that she did not want him to live with her against his will - but her object in coming to London was to be fully satisfied as to whether he was married or not; the young woman was very civil and had all the appearance of a respectable person; of course she was very much distressed we made her as comfortable as we could and in the Evening went with her to Mrs Mason's who had promised to procure a Lodging for her. Latham agreed to set up 10s if we would advance it to her, to pay her passage down again - the poor creature was very much distressed scarcely holding up her head all the day long - she told us she had been married to him for 6 years and was only 22 yrs of age now that they had no family and that she had been in service several years having been 3 years at the situation she now held. I never before witnessed such a case and they who could withold their sympathy and relief to a fellow creature so unfortunately circumstanced was unworthy the name of human and destitute of the noblest feelings of our nature:— walked out in the Evening - came home about 10 and am ready for bed - a very fine day. - P.S. Have said more upon this subject than appears necessary but think at some time the case may be brought forward in a Court of Justice and I therefore have noted it more particularly.

Monday October 21   Rose about 8 A M after breakfast much to my surprise Latham presented his Marriage Certificate to me - which showed that he was married as Wm F Latham Widower to Ann Flynne Widow at St. Anns' Blackfriars (I think in the month of February of the present year), signed by the Minister (Curate) and Witnesses, he appeared quite unconcerned about any consequences which might ensue, saw the young woman at Mrs. Masons in the Evening & gave her 10s which Latham agreed to pay to me again; she proposes going out by a steamer tomorrow morning:— went to Borrodailes in the afternoon to order the Beaver and received it a short time after walked out in the evening and lost a silk pocket handcherchief - I suppose it was taken out of my pocket while going thro' a crowd which had assembled around some men who were quarrelling - had a glass of ale at the Two Brewers - came home and am ready for bed 11 o'clock P M promised to see the young woman get on the packet in the morning another fine day.

Tuesday October 22   Did not rise till 8 A M having quite forgot my promise to see Lathams wife off the packet sails at 8, but learned from Mrs. Mason that she was gone, one of her boys accompanying her to the Vessel - Button, another silk man met them at the Wharf and saw her get on board and the vessel sail:— the Morning Chronicle of this day announced the death of Henry Lord

Brougham[86] he having been thrown out of a carriage by the axletree breaking was kicked by one of the horses and a wheel passing over his head killed him on the spot - the Editor very kindly and very justly bewails his death, altho' his recent political conduct has been such as to cause many of his most ardent admirers to swerve from him; but still a grateful people will deeply lament the awful death of the man who has so long and so successfully battled in their cause - and whatever his eccentricities was unquestionably the greatest man of his age - and posterity will recount his many glorious victories over corruption and bigotry and tyranny; with a fervour which will render his name great and blessed by countless myriads yet unborn - I personally grieve for him - tho' his late policy was not what we expected from him, but how can I fathom the objects of his gigantic mind perhaps what appeared to us like perversness or treachery; might be only a better mode of attaining some valuable privelege for the well being of the people; for let what may be said; he devoted the best part of his unequalled energies to that hallowed object. - received a pack from home - no letter for me - the day has been fine but the Evening indicates rain, wind S.W.

Wedensday October 23   Rose at 7 - heard in the morning that the rumour of the death of Lord Brougham was false, am very glad its so, for we are deeply indebted to him as a nation and I hope yet to see him pursue the same glorious career which won for him a nations' love, and would have rendered his death (at this time) a national calamity; for the Mechanic & the Manufacturer; the Philospher & the (Liberal) Politician have all partook of the ample stores of his rich mind & his never failing application of them to some good purpose tho his later actions have not been pleasing to very many of his early friends and admirers - wet in the Afternoon.

Thursday October 24   Rose about 7 - steamed 6 silk shells before breakfast and intend to learn the branch of silk hat making acting upon my old motto that whatever useful thing I learn it is in addition to my little stock of knowledge and may be at some time available; but at any rate it never can be injurious - performed the other parts necessary to their completion as bodies in the course of the day and they were pronounced by J.I. to be done well; at this I was much pleased for tho' many people similarly circumstanced to myself would scorn the idea of descending to so lowly a pursuit,[87] this feeling did not actuate me, who was influenced by the motives before stated, remembering as I do the story of the 'basket maker', the day has been a thorough wet one - nothing else of particular importance - 11 P M ready for bed.

Friday October 25   Rose about 7 - sent 2 pack 3 doz Bls to my Father - enclosed a cheque for £4 16s 6d and a letter to my Parents concerning James coming to London this has been a thorough wet day - fine and cold in the Evening.

Part III

January 1st. 1843 Sunday The propriety and utility of Keeping a Diary wherein to record events of private and public interest appearing to be supported by every day's experience besides the great pleasure received in referring to the notes in the former pages - induce me to make another attempt, in the belief that my more intimate acquaintance with business will prevent me being so much annoyed as to interrupt this useful project and also that many of the foibles which before diverted my attention possess no claims to turn me aside, therefore do I think it likely that in this instance success is probable, for I shall not attempt too minute an account but merely note the most striking events of a general and personal nature:— with this view I shall proceed to observe upon this first day of the year which has been very fine for the weather and very pleasant to me socially - breakfasted immediately wash'd & went out with the intention of going to Surry Chapel[88] but conflicting feelings chequed any pur- pose - walkd home to dinner after which I went to Clapham to take a Nonconformist paper[89] to Mr Embleton - he expected me to dinner took dessert and wine with him, afterwards Tea & Supper - I was much pleased to see him so happy and comfortable, & contrasted his position the fruit of his skill, his industry and his economy with that of the reckless many who dissipate their means to the injury of their persons and so impair their circumstances that a miserable existence is often dragged on by means of others bounty or charity - also with the extravagant spendthrift who in a few years consumes as much as would with prudent management have been an ample provision for his whole life, whilst his excesses have reduced him to the lowest depths of want and misery - not so however with Mr. E - he spends frugally what he has acquired industriously - his house bespeaks plenty and contentment - his practice appears well qualified for domestic duties and for companionship - I thought he was especially blessed in his reflections and associations and considered him an admirable model, well worthy of imitation; he and Mrs. E. were both very kind to me, it was amongst the happiest of my days especially since my residence here; left Clapham at ½ past 9 walked home by ½ past 10 - the Evening - very starlight and frosty - the day had been mild & sunny more like the weather of April than new years day -

January 2/43 Monday Rose at 7 weather very frosty, looked out 2 doz hats for Moule of Reading - ordered 15 lbs of Beaver at Whitings & Dixons & 15 lbs of Nut. bade money 3/9 per lb at some (Prices Bro. 81/- White 100/- Nutria 19/- Bks 11/-) Sax wool. called on Ellwoods for David,[90] they would not give me work at present but took his address and promised to send if anything transpired to favor such course received a letter dated 31/12/42 from E.C. - received a pack from Dronfield of 9 Doz 44B bodies enclosing a pie for me and my top coat, walk'd over into the City nearly to the Town - call'd at Wheelers [91] on my return smoked a pipe, drank a glass of gin water, came home & am now ready for bed 11 P M. Weather very clear & frosty.

Tuesday 1 Month 3rd 43   Rose at ½ past 7. supplied every man with work by 11 A M gave out a dye of hats - after dinner weigh'd out a pack to send to Dronfield - received a letter from David in the morning which gave me great pleasure in knowing that I had a Brother capable of feeling and writing the sentiments it contained, in it there is much matter for grave reflection - was anxiously expecting a note from E.C. but as none came I went out at 8 P M to the Surry Chapel - there heard an eloquent address from Dr Cummins on the necessity of exertions to Missionarize China - altho' eloquent it was evasive full of abuse of the Catholics - laudatory of the result of the war with china & condemnatory of its origin - I consider him a talkative fellow of undefined principle - save the one of getting money to support his particular party for he said not a word about the Established Church with her immense means of neglecting the duty which he showed as a nation devolved upon us, but, that the London Missionary Society alone was prepared to take advantage of the favourable opportunity for spreading Christianity in China - walk'd home with Miss Kennay - but did not go into the house met J. Philips with whom I went to smoke a pipe had 1 pint ½ & ½ came home now ½ past 11 - ready for bed, very frosty.

Wedensday 1st Month 4th 43   Rose ½ past 7 wrote to [*Blank*] stating my views rather positively - after breakfast recd a note from [*Blank*] enquiring if the one of Saturday had reached me - wrote again in the forenoon further elucidating my views - received a reply to my first a little before 9 - went down to M St. as requested, spent a very pleasant Evening had some very serious conversation staid until past 12 and agreed to walk down to the Elephant by 8 tomorrow Evening weather not so cold and inclined to change from frost to rain - 1 o'clock now for bed.

Thursday 5th   Rose at 8 - received 2 Carboys of Vitriol from Evans' Brothers - returned 2 Empties - J. Jackson called on me before breakfast so took his with me - paid Jno. Pattersons' Account and ordered a hat for himself; he brought me a few cigars a present from Mr Harvey - wrote to Stephenson, went to the Elephant according to appointment, thence to M St. spent a very pleasant Evening returned at ½ past 12 - Weather windy & frosty - ordered 1 gross of persian sides of Mr Cousins:—

Friday 6th   Rose at ½ past 7 - post brought pretty good orders from Mr I & J. S.[92]   which I soon got into play - being very eager in consequence of the length of time we have done nothing - received two Carboys of Turps (Stringer & Booty price 3/- wt retd 2 empties - also 1 gro persian Sides from D. Walters price 36/- Walked down to the Elephant, thence to the Swan Dover Road, met Chas

69

Howe, with whom I went to the Roebuck, came away at ½ past 11 - weather frosty. -

Saturday 7th 1843 Went thro' the usual routine of business; sent a note to [*Blank*] called on Jarratt at the request of David did not see him, left word I would call on Monday - wrote to David, Mr W. Wilson[93] called on me to assist them in raising a subscription for the Anti Corn Law League, which I relunctantly undertook - looked all day for a note from E.C. but was disappointed walked nearly to C. Gate,[94] returned home to see the late Post, delivered nothing for me. Much concerned went to Wheelers' staid 'till nearly 12 - Mr. Rusby had inquired for me there, weather cold & frosty. -

Sunday 1 Month 8th 1843 Rose early went to Surry Chapel in the morning - Mr Sherman preached - was too late to hear the text, but suppose it was 'God is our refuge and our strength, a very present help in time of trouble' - the subject was ably treated but I cannot say it was profitable to me, my mind was too much engaged with the disappointments of the last two days, saw [*Blank*] after the service, she gave me a note which Miss K had brought to our house on Saturday Evening during my short absence, walked round by C. Green,[95] had some serious conversation respecting the aspect of our personal affairs which caused much unpleasant feeling but which I continued to hide and spoke very cheerfully - was promised a note on Monday morning, we parted at ¼ to 3, - came home dined off cold meat & bread, went to Golden Lane to give up some tickets, called for a minute or two at 55 O.B.[96] wishing to see Kelsey - he was not there, Came to S. Chapel at 6 o'clock Mr Sherman again preached from the 13th Chapter of the Gospel of St. Matthew - the parable of the sower, - my attention was more fixed than in the Morning - and I thought peculiarly happy in illustrating the various thoughts which occupied our minds during service, which he compared to the thorns which sprung up and choked the seed, also the manner of the wicked one spoken of verse 19th - how he induced some to sleep, others to criticise, some to apply the different parts to their neighbors, others to procrastinate - some to be too vain of their own talents to acknowleddge any superior, and many to consider, worship nothing more than a form of respectability; he concluded a most able discourse, by exhorting all to eagerly embrace the truths of Christianity thus to fortify themselves against the wiles of the wicked one who is always trying to 'catch away that which was sown in our hearts' - I hope the discourse was to me profitable - Walked down Blackfriars Road with Miss K. met [*Blank*] went to Mt St, supped there, had another long chat, agreed to meet at S. Chapel tomorrow Evening - I am anxious to make an end of this matter, but *most* anxious for it in the manner I have so long wished and anticipated. ¼ to 1.

Monday 9th Pursued my usual avocations thro' the day, in the Evening met

70

Miss K who stated the cause of *[Blank]* absence, walked as far as East Lane returning met Jno. Charlton called at the Artichoke for half an hour came home - very gloomy - Morning very fine & frosty Evening a rough wind & heavy rain - now to bed ¼ past 10.

Tuesday 10th Received a letter from David, also one from Mr Scott from Taunton to which I replied telling him of the unpleasantness I had had with H. S.[97] - who refused to pay me for pane of glass which I had sent for during his absence of two hours on Monday Afternoon went with Jackson & Rusby into the City. Rusby gave me 10s towards the 'League Fund' - came home ½ past 12

Wedensday 11th Nothing worth noting in business: received a note from E. - to which I sent a reply, went to the Chartist Meeting in the Evening & afterwards walked with Ratcliffe nearly to East Lane returned at ½ past 11. snow & rain in the Evening very cold during the day -

Thursday 12th Went in the forenoon to E. Coopers' who spoke pretty freely & clearly upon the state of our business and the prospects of the concern, all he said accorded with my opinions so far as I knew the subject but he named several things which were new to me: — wrote Scott in the Evening to Plymouth - Mr. Nall called a little past 8 with whom I went to hear a lecture on the Corn Laws, the subject was cleverly handled by the Lecturer 'Timothy Falvey'[98] an Irishman & Artisan from Manchester or Macclesfield - his perspicuity and sound argument were well calculated to convince an audience of the necessity of their abolition - Weather fine and windy had been boisterous the preceding night. Sharp frost at night. 11 o'clock wind changed to South West. Much warmer

Friday 13th Looked anxiously for the Post, no letters from T.I. or J.S. - this rather damped my spirits for it is now a week since they sent any order: Received a note from E - about 5, returned an answer immediately with a request - spent the Evening at Mr Nalls' - came home ½ past 10 - a wet night and greater part of the day. Wind high evening - fine.

Saturday 14th Rose at ½ past 6 - walked round Newgate Market in which were hundreds of Pigs & chiefly very good pork - No order per Post only one letter for H.S. from J.S. Plymouth sent off Withers' goods - received a note from E - stating the impossibility of my request being complied with & reckoned early called on Jarratt (for David) but did not see him - sat alone till past 8 when Jackson called - we went together to Wheelers' staid till 11 - a rough day with rain & snow rather frosty the snow remains on the roofs - Jackson sleeps with me tonight.

Sunday 1 Month 15th, 1843 Rose at 7 - Jackson left me after breakfast. I went to Surrey Chapel came home to dinner (Irish Stew) after dinner walked to

Peckham with much difficulty found Mr Rittson who walked with me to Kent Road, called at the Dun Cow, staid till 9 P M conversing chiefly about the prospect of our concern, he entered into the matter with much feeling considering himself victimised between the principal and a subordinate, and expressed his belief that a just Providence would require retribution; - called at Duffields on my return but would not stay, got home at 10 and am now off to bed - frosty and fine moonlight - no fire and all the usual domestic inconveniences.

Monday 16th Received orders from Mr. Scott from Barnstaple nothing from Mr I & a Sheffield Independent, from G Ward also a letter from Brother Jim; gave an order to Mr Hoyle of Manchester for 6 Gros. Sides at 8/3 two samples of Cloth for patches at 5/6 & 6/6 - 6 yds each went to Surrey Chapel in the Evening met [Blank] walked to M. S. had a curious conversation which will require my serious consideration, left about ½ past 11 - came direct home saw a great fire about ½ past 7 in the South East.[99] Mr Rusby called for a few minutes - weather warm & disposed to wet -

Tuesday 1 Month 17th Rose at 7 - no letter from Mr I that I know of - saw in the Morning Chronicle that the Bank of Parker, Shore & Co of Sheffield had suspended payments [100] — Mr. Walker of Leawood called and presented his account but kindly observed it might not be convenient to pay it just now - learned that the fire I saw on the previous Evening was at a large Floor Cloth manufactory in Old Kent Road damages £20,000 - Jackson called in the Evening with whom I went about 9 P M to the Rotunda[101] to hear Mr Buckingham [102] lecture on the Corn Laws, a crowded meeting but the Lecture nearly concluded when we arrived, called at the Queens Head - in the Evening I stumped 1 doz Jerry bodies for blk Shells, received a pack from home but did not open it - weather warm with indications of rain - am now going to write E - then off to bed - Wrote G. Ward to ascertain whether Parker & Shores suspension would affect them.

Wedensday 18th 1843 Rose early. Mr. Irwin came in from his journey, I thought he looked very ill and care worn, received a letter from Brother Jim informing me of Parker & Shores Bank stopping and some of its consequences in Dronfield also one from Mr Scott from Plymouth - where, he said 7 or 8 vessels were driven ashore by the hurricame and tiles 'flew about like bricks' [103] - wrote to E did not sent the note I wrote last night:— Jno. Bryson called in the afternoon met him again in the Evening in Long Lane Smithfield & took him a Doz hoods which had been sent for him from Dronfield & with them his Account total £6 19s 6¾d due to them at home £4 1s 6d - Mr Rusby accompanied me came home about 11 - weather quite warm.

Thurday 19th Rose at 8 - assisted Mr I to look out his orders which were few & small, received a note from [Blank] about ½ past 8 - saw an Advertisement in the Chronicle which I thought was from a party I know for a situation as Governess - saying the party 'was quite competent good tempered and very fond of children' - Address - at Mr Murphys 116 Holborn [104] - walked out after business (which kept me till ½ past 9) as far as St. Georges Ch. [105] - got home ¼ past 10 and am now ready to retire to rest; - whilst my most particular friend is indulging at the Adelaide Gallery [106] - weather quite warm like *Spring*.

Friday 20th Rose at 5 weighd 4 Ruffs with 2 dz Nut. Side and 2 Clippings, bowed them before breakfast received 3 letters from Mr Scott, Geo. Ward, & David - answered Mr Scotts to the Crown Hotel. Southampton - George says 'Sheffield was never before in such an uproar as on Monday & Tuesday in consequence of the Bank Stopping - Sheaf works & many other places immediately closed' - 'tis supposed, there will not be much loss, their £5 notes are fetching £4.10 to £4.15 Mr O. Shore is said to have advanced £150,000 within the last 4 yrs to sustain the Credit of the Bank the Morning Advertiser says in its City Article that the Liabilities are £600,000 assetts £725,000 chiefly in advances to Merchants & Manufacturers but from the bad state of things cannot realize their securities, & ascribe it to restricted Commerce which prevents the Americans paying their heavy debts to Sheffield Merchants in produce' which they have the means to do and are anxious to do but the cursed Aristocratic Protection is allowed to destroy every other interest in the Kingdom wrote to [Blank] Jackson spent an hour with me in the Evening left about ¼ to 10 - now for rest for I'm tired - Fine & warm -

Saturday 21st Rose at 6 - could not get to my ruffing because of having some greasy dregs so was obliged to have the kettle fire drawn about noon - drew 7£ on my account - Enclosed a balance of £1 12s 6d to Davenport & Sons, Chesterfield the proceeds of some tame Rabbit skins sent in the beginning of last year had got part of them carrotted & cut but sent the stuff with a dye of hats we had done for them - reckoned between 5 & 6 the few people we have employed all had better wages this week than for a long time previous which gave me much satisfaction - after supper Miss K. called with a note from [Blank] agreeable to the instructions of which I walked over to the Times' Office a place I had never before seen from thence walked to Camberwell Gate & up to Denmark Hill:— the morning papers contain an account of a Mr Drummond Sec. to Sir [Robert] Peel being shot yesterday.[107]

Wrote to David in Post time & gave it as my opinion that he must send Jarretts bodies told him not to be too precipitate in going to house in Dronfield as he spoke before about coming to London - received 5s of the Makers which I advanced to them when they were in great distress at the latter end of October, also 2s 6d from Latham leaving his debt - 16s 6d - Weather fine.

Sunday 1 Month 22nd 1843 Rose at ½ past 7 - went to Surrey Chapel, after service walked toward home with [Blank] dined at a house in Walworth Road of Veal, Pork, plain pudding, greens & potatoes & bread all for 8d gave the girl 2d for it was the cheapest dinner I had ever had away from home - Went with [Blank] up Camberwell Grove down to Goose Green, thence to Peckham Rye - through Peckham, returned by Camberwell Green promised to be at S. C. [108] in the Evening if I could get away from Brysons' in time - went there in a bus took tea & supper for I found myself necessitated to stay longer than I at first intended left about ½ past 10, walked home in ¾ of an hour, removed the mare & am now ready for bed regretting that my previous engagement deprived me of the society in which I could have spent the Evening more happily - tho' Brysons uniform kindness has always rendered the time spent with him & family particularly pleasant.

Monday 23rd Rose at 8 - received Independent from Geo. Ward - two small orders from Mr Scott - looked out 9 doz of hats - wrote to George & in the Evening to [Blank] I think Mr I looks very dispirited and feel very much grieved for him - he must make some great alteration either by increasing his business or reducing his expenses or certain ruin awaits him - had a pint of ale at Mrs Stonars came home at 10 - and am now off to bed - Fine thro' the day but offers to rain now -

Tuesday 24th [No entry]

Wedensday 25 Opened a parcel from Hoyle & Newbury Manchester - find by the Evg papers that Mr Drummond died at ½ past 10 this morning - all persons regret his death.

Thursday 26th [No entry]

Friday 27th Mr Scott returned from the West journey trade no better, received a note from [Blank] went with Mr S in the Evening to Stonar's and afterwards walked with him to St. Georges' Church, came home at ¼ to 11 - now ready for bed. paid Mr Scott a sovereign which I owed him. -

Saturday 28th Received a letter from Cousin T. Jenkinson & one from Jim, am sorry to learn that Tom is very unwell and not likely to be able to follow the business again soon, he promises to send me a 'Sheffield Iris' - went in the Evening to Blkfriars Road and after that had a great deal of walking to & fro, between there & Camberwell Gate. got home at 12 - Weather fine -

Sunday 29th Walked after breakfast round St. Georges fields, [109] came home to dinner, Afterwards went down Blkfriars Road and met [Blank] & [Blank] when they had dined we all three got into a bus and rode to Regents' Park, walked thence to Primrose Hill, the day fine and the prospect beautiful, refreshed at Chalk Farm came back thro' Camden town, got a 'bus at the York and Albany - rode to the New Cut, left my Company there and walked to Ratcliffes' where I staid the remainder of the Evening until 10 o'clock called on [Blank] and had some rather unpleasant feeling, created by what appeared to me invidious remarks - came home about 11 - day very fine quite spring.

Monday 30th   Rose at ½ past 5 and wrote a long note to E - declining an interview which had been agreed to on Sunday - was very unhappy all day - did not go out in the Evening - agreed to meet Mr Scott tomorrow morning to see him off by a Hull Steamer [110]   for the North Journey weather fine - wrote to George Ward & my Father.

Tuesday 31st   Afternoon went to weigh a pack to send to Dronfield had not quite done when Mr. George Booth of Denton called upon me, just as we were leaving a note from E. arrived, informing me that 'I had taken a much more enlarged view of the observations made than they were intended to furnish' went with Booth to Wheelers' thence to Gerrard's Hall,[111]   he very kindly told me that if I should be in want of a situation which the state of affairs here seemed to indicate he should be very glad to treat with me, - I did not mention my opinion of our affairs, he told me he had heard it from respectable parties since he had been in London that we could not long go on as we were, I felt very pleased by his kindness, altho' his offer does not accord with my present views - weather fine left him at one A M - saw Mr Scott off by the Water witch in the morning & bought a fish at Billingsgate.

Wedensday February 1st   Rose at 8 - found myself much the worse for the little indulgence of last night tho' it was not at all excessive, wrote to [Blank] explaining mine of Monday; got off a pack for Dronfield, - towards Evening became very unwell and was obliged to lie down, whilst Mr Rusby was present; got to bed at ½ past 9.

Thursday 2nd   Parliament was this day opened by Commission the speech from the Throne was if possible worse for its want of meaning than many which have preceded it - a piece of humbug about our *Victories* - in China & Affghanistan [112]   and a hope that prosperity at home would be one of the results, but no mention of any other step to be taken to produce such prosperity - I think the Leaguers will now see that a Parliament of Monopolists is not hardly the thing to remove the Monopolies by which they live, surely they may now see that the only thing which can be done is to effectually change the system and restore the house of Commons to its legitimate owners the people - weather set in very cold so that the temperature of the weather and of politics seemed to become chilled at the same time - Snow, rain & wind in the Evening.

Friday 3rd   Received a note granting an interview as I had requested - time not fixed, sent Dan with a reply - afterwards walked down to M. St. spent a very pleasant Evening - the weather intensely cold - Peel says he does not contemplate any change in the Corn Laws, but says also he does not bind himself to the present one.

Saturday 4th Hung about all day with little or nothing to do - T. I. did not come near all day wrote to Geo. Ward telling him how things looked here. Mr Rusby & myself went to Stonar's in the Evening very rough & wet & cold weather with frost & snow - came home at 11 -

Sunday 5th Rose early, washed & dressed before breakfast walk round St. Georges' fields, and on the Boro - home again a good deal annoyed by a little circumstance which occurred in the Morning took another walk before dinner which I had at Wheelers staid there till near four o'clock then walked to Chapham round the common called at Mr Embletons chatted several hours took supper and a glass of brandy & water with him, left there at 10 - fine frosty night got home at 11 - our conversation was a good deal about our concern, he promised to speak to T. I. about it - this needs to be done by some friend -

Monday 6th Weigh'd off some Sax, Wool & Beaver from Whitings & Dixon. - after business took a walk down London Road, and there fell in with [*Blank*] walked home with them, had some more of the old sort of chat & came away at 11 - frosty but rather disposed to wet. received a letter from Sister Mary,[113] who I find is learning dressmaking -

Tuesday 7th Received a letter from Platts [114] & one from J. Turner: – at 5 P.M. went to the Tea party and Ball given at Baxters' Union St [115] to assist in paying the expenses of the Delegation to the Birmingham Conference.[116] F. O'Connor [117] in the Chair Self in Vice Chair, Barstow & Cleave [118] were present and also addressed the meeting all went off tolerably well - dancing commenced at 9 - I was not much pleased with that part of the entertainment, fell in with Miss Clarke [119] who had accompanied Mr & Mrs Ratcliffe staid till nearly 4, Wednesday morning and then walked home with Ratcliffe & party, took tea and staid till nearly 6 - found Mayes had opened the premises so I walked off to bed for an hour or two.

Wedensday 8th Rose at 9 - quite well pursued the usual course of business thro' the day, went to the Bro. Bear for ½ an hour at night, returned at 10 - received a message about 7 --- I this day considered much on the propriety of taking any further steps in the Political Agitation of the Country finding that my efforts & my sacrifices which have been by no means small for my circumstances, were not likely to produce a corresponding amount of public good, I have thought it most prudent to withdraw from the Active part for the present still believing firmly in the correctness of my views; but deem it best to wait until more see the same way that then a simultaneous effort of greater numbers might break shackles which bind us and throw off the yoke of the oppressor - besides the state of things in our establishment is such as requires the more undivided attention to prepare for what may ensue.

Thursday 9th   Rose at 7 - Mr I has not been at business this day at all, what can this mean? - more & more do I see the propriety of preparing for consequences, also of the resolve I made yesterday - did not go out at all.

Friday 10th   Mrs Irwin came in the morning & informed us that Governor was seriously ill, he was taken on Wednesday Evening and was in bed most of the day on Thursday - his medical adviser ordered him to go to bed again this morning, his complaint is a kind of fever arising from colds - and also an affaction of the liver - went in the Evening to Walker & Gordons and to Airds but could not get an order from either them call'd at Wheelers' on my return, got home at 11 - received 5 Hogsheads of Plates from Bowkers[120]   prices, 3s 10d 4s 6d, 5s 6d - dont know what we shall do with them for in reality we have no trade - sent off Per Rail to Spencer Bath 4 hats 1 [size] 7 $\frac{5}{8}$ 2 [size] 7 $\frac{1}{2}$ 1 [size] 7 $\frac{3}{8}$ - the only ones since Tuesday Noon - this can never do! received a note from fin.

Saturday 11th   Looked out plates to complete 3 small orders which had been waiting, and got them off. heard from Slyfield that Governor was rather better last night, and spoke of coming up on Monday reckoned between 4 & 5 - wrote to David saying a word or two on the state of things here - Mr Embleton kindly invited me to dine with him tomorrow.

Notes to the Diary

1. William Cobbett's *Advice to Young Men and (incidentally) to Young Women* was first published in fourteen parts and issued in paper wrappers. The last letter is dated 25 August, 1830. Cobbett died in 1835.

2. This seems to be a quotation from a translation of Pythagoras's *Golden Verses.*

3. See Appendix III for details of local people.

4. Methodist Missionary Sermons: Joseph went to the 19th annual meeting of the Methodist Auxiliary Missionary Society held at Carver Street Chapel on 22 April and Ebenezer Chapel, Moorfields on 23 April with James Montgomery in the chair. Preachers at services on Sunday 21 April at Carver Street included Mr Dawson at 3p.m. and the Rev. Jabez Bunting at 6.30p.m. (*Sheffield Iris,* 16 April 1833).

5. Ebenezer Wesleyan Chapel, Moorfields, Sheffield, erected 1823.

6. Rev. Jabez Bunting, D.D.: an eloquent Yorkshire local preacher, appointed to the Carver Street Circuit and a President of the Methodist Conference,(J. Holland and J. Everett, *Memoirs of the life and writings of James Montgomery* (1854), vol. V, p. 129; *Carver Street Methodist Church, 1805-1955*, 1955).

7. William Dawson: a Methodist celebrity, 'the eccentric, but excellent and famed local preacher . . . like no other man . . .' (*Methodist Records; or, selections from the Journal of . . . A. Lynn*, ed. J. Stokoe, 1858).

8. Introduction, note 19.

9. *Sheffield Iris* newspaper.

10. Sir William Ingilby Bt, 1783-1854, was a Reformer and was inclined towards Radicalism; M.P. for Lincolnshire, 1823-35, he was in favour of protection for the farmer.

11. The tax on malt was condemned for making it too costly for the poorer classes to brew their own beer and ale, thus driving them to the fast growing number of beer-houses.

12. Lord Althorp, 1782-1845, became 3rd Earl Spencer, a Whig and Leader of the House of Commons in 1830, Chancellor of the Exchequer 1830-34. Melbourne said of him that he was 'the tortoise on whose back the world reposes'.

13. Introduction, note 27.

14. Introduction, note 18.

15. Introduction, note 18.

16. Sir John Key, 1794-1858, M.P. for City of London 1833.

17. Manor House, Dronfield (now the County Library); built by Ralph Burton *c*.1700.

18. Oliver Goldsmith, 'The Deserted Village'.

19. Sunday School.

20. Introduction, p. 9. .

21. Joseph says 'Larcum' but the reference is to the Rev. Charles Larom, minister of the Baptist church, Townhead Street, Sheffield, 1821-66. A separate Baptist church was created in Dronfield in 1846 when 14-15 members of the Independent congregation asked to be transferred to Mr. Larom's pastoral care (F. M. Sanderson, *History of Dronfield Baptist Church*, 1946).

22. For all hatmaking and manufacturing firms see Appendix II.

23. This refers to the Birmingham Political Union, founded by Thomas Attwood (see note 34 below); it was the most influential radical organisation in the country *c*.1833.

24. Sir John Cam Hobhouse, 1786-1869, created Lord Broughton; Radical politician and friend of Byron; M.P. in 1820 and President of the Board of Control, 1835-41; invented the phrase 'His Majesty's Opposition'.

25. Introduction, note 18.

26. Col. George de Lacy Evans, 1787-1870; entered Parliament as a Radical in 1830; served in India and the Peninsular War; was in the Waterloo campaign and later commanded a division in the Crimea, wounded at the battle of the Alma; knighted 1837.

27. William Paley, Archdeacon of Carlisle; wrote many works on evidences of Christianity, moral and political philosophy, sermons, texts and advice to clergy. Edmund Paley published *The Works of William Paley, With Additional Sermons and a Corrected Account of the Life and Writings of the Author* (1825).

28. Probably *Bell's Weekly Messenger*, a conservative paper with a large circulation dealing with politics, general news, *belles lettres* and fine arts.

29. Rev. Isaac Watts, 1674-1748, hymn writer etc; his *Improvement of the Mind* was published in 1741 as a supplement to his *Logick or the Right Use of Reason* (1725).

30. Introduction, note 17.

31. Introduction, note 22.

32. Also called Spa Fields and the site of a prison; the meeting referred to was called by the National Union of Working Classes, hoping to form a National Convention. *Sheffield Iris*, 21 May 1833 reported upwards of 2,000 people present.

33. Report *Sheffield Iris*, 27 May 1833.

34. Thomas Attwood, 1783-1856, a banker and ironmaster of Birmingham who was active 1830-32 in the national petition in support of the Charter; he became disillusioned with the Reform Act of 1832; he called a meeting for May 1833 saying 'Once more in your countless thousands masses come with me with the hearts of lions but the gentleness of lambs . . . meet again at Newhall Hill'.

35. Daniel O'Connell, 1775-1847; called to the Irish Bar in 1798; he addressed the mass meeting in Birmingham on 20 May 1833, which protested against the Government's Irish policy as well as attacking it for refusing to extend the suffrage and for being hostile to the interests of the working classes.

36. Henry Peter Brougham, Lord Brougham and Vaux, 1778-1868; an advocate in 1800 and founder of the Edinburgh Review; M.P. in 1810, Lord Rector of Edinburgh University in 1825 and Lord Chancellor 1830-34; distrusted by Whigs who were jealous of his Parliamentary reputation; said by Greville to lack 'ballast' for his talents.

37. Possibly connected with the Friendly Sick Club at Dronfield (records at DRO).

38. Introduction, note 18.

39. Letter from Ebenezer Elliott to the editor of the *Morning Chronicle*, answering editorial comments made on a speech by Elliott on 20 May 1833. Reply from the editor printed in the *Sheffield Iris*, 4 June 1833. See also Introduction, note 17.

40. Associated with Dronfield parish church feast day, 24 June.

41. Upper Chapel, Norfolk Street, Sheffield was Unitarian. Nether Chapel, erected 1715, was Independent, demolished 1826 and a new chapel built. The minister in 1833 was Rev. Thomas Smith, a classical tutor at Rotherham Independent College. The Wesleyans also had a chapel in Norfolk Street, enlarged in 1833 and holding 1,600. It may have been this one which Joseph attended; the Mr Allen referred to was superintendent at the New Connexion's chapel in Scotland Street. (*White's Sheffield Directory*, 1833).

42. Preacher from Bolton.

43. The mother church of Carver Street Chapel was Norfolk Street Wesleyan Chapel. In

1831 Carver Street became head of the Sheffield West Circuit and Norfolk Street of Sheffield East. It may have been this chapel which was known as the Old Church or Joseph may have meant Sheffield Parish Church, now the Cathedral.

44. Introduction, note 19.

45. Thomas Gisbourne, M.P. for North Derbyshire, 1832-37.

46. Edward George Stanley, 14th Earl of Derby, 1799-1869, moderate supporter of Parliamentary reform; as Colonial Secretary carried an Act for abolition of slavery.

47. Introduction, note 18.

48. The predecessor of the present Roman Catholic church of St Marie was also in Norfolk Row, Sheffield.

49. Presumably Joseph gave the bride away.

50. Probably Hardhurst Bank, Unstone, formerly a steep rocky bank on the turnpike road; a bridge now carries the road over the railway at this point.

51. Possibly Sharrow Head House, at the junction of Sharrow Lane and Cemetery Road, Sheffield.

52. The diary, 25 Jan. 1843, mentions Hoyle and Newbury of Manchester and on 16 Jan. 1843 refers to Mr Hoyle of Manchester. Edward Hoyle was probably a business connection of Irwin's.

53. Introduction, note 39.

54. Introduction, note 31.

55. Thames Steamboat Towing Co.'s tugboat *Samson* (*Times*, 3 Sep. 1839).

56. Stringfellow and Davenport were manufacturing hatters in Chesterfield.

57. Not identified.

58. Hatmaking terms are explained in Appendix I.

59. See Appendix II.

60. John Irwin.

61. Scott and Rittson were travellers for Irwin. Rittson was later dismissed for drunkeness on the road (JWC, letter 30 Oct. 1840).

62. Joseph's brother, James, born 1818, aged 21 in 1839.

63. Fuller's, 96 Long Lane, Southwark, for whom Joseph worked after 1843.

64. Introduction, note 38.

65. Public house on Borough High Street, Southwark. (*Tallis's London Street Views*, 1839).

66. An engineer; see Introduction, pp. 17-18.

67. Southwark Bridge, erected 1814-19 under the direction of Rennie; the central span of 240 feet was the largest in the world at that time. (W. Westall and S. Owen, *Picturesque Tour of the River Thames*, 1828).

68. Introduction, note 38.

69. Isaac Watts's *Logick, or the Right Use of Reason* was first published in 1725.

70. P. Murphy's *Weather Almanac*, 1838; he wrote other books on weather, climate and

astronomy (information kindly supplied by the National Meteorological Library, Bracknell).

71. Harriatt, born 1824, aged 15 in 1839.

72. Liberals were exhorted to rejoice over his defeat, which brought an end to civil war in Spain.

73. Mercurous chloride, formerly used as a purgative.

74. Probably the counting house or office clerk.

75. Tropical American tree (*haematoxylon campechianum*) of the Caesalpina family; its heartwood is dark red and is used in dyeing; it is exported in logs.

76. West of Chesterfield, now usually called New Brampton.

77. James Ivyleafe, hatter and manufacturer, 139 Regent Street, London (*Pigot's Commercial Directory*, 1839).

78. Bryson is also mentioned on 18 and 22 Jan. 1843.

79. Off Old Kent Road.

80. St Olave's Lodge was one of the oldest in the Unity of Oddfellows and one of the largest.

81. Introduction, note 50.

82. The women were often employed as tippers.

83. The October Fair was held on the first Thursday after 12 October (*Derbyshire Courier*, 19 Oct. 1840). Fairs were also held in March and April for the sale of horses, sheep and cattle.

84. A young lad, Hawes, aged 15, whose father had died insane, jumped from the same place as a young woman only a week previously. The Monument attracted those bent on self-destruction. (*The Times*, 13 and 21 Sept. 1839).

85. An employee at Irwin's; also mentioned on 21 Jan. 1843.

86. See note 36.

87. See Introduction, p. 18.

88. Surrey Chapel, a large brick octagonal building on Blackfriars Road, built 1784; one of the largest in London, holding 3,000. (*London as it is To-day: Where to Go and What to See During the Great Exhibition*, 1851).

89. Probably the *Nonconformist Magazine;* it was edited by Edward Miall and supported the Complete Suffrage Union. Miall wrote a series of articles in 1841 on the reconciliation of the middle and labouring classes. The magazine was severely criticised by Matthew Arnold later in the century for its picture of the ideal life - 'jealousy of the Establishment, disputes, tea meetings, openings of chapels, sermons . . .' (cf. Asa Briggs, *The Age of Improvement* (1969), chapter 6).

90. Joseph's younger brother, at this time working in Dronfield as a hatter.

91. Unidentified.

92. Mr Irwin and J. Scott.

93. William Wilson, reported in *The Times,* 16 Jan. 1843, as moving a resolution at a meeting in the Literary and Scientific Institute, Borough Road, Southwark, at which Chartists tried to involve the League speakers in discussion.

94. Camberwell Gate.

95. Camberwell Green.

96. Old Borough.

97. Probably Slyfield.

98. Introduction, note 46.

99. Messrs Gounston and Roll's floor cloth manufactory. *Sheffield Iris,* 21 Jan. 1843 gives the damage as £50,000 and two factories totally destroyed.

100. A meeting in Sheffield's Cutlers' Hall on 16 Jan. 1843 expressed unabated confidence in other banks in the town to prevent a run on them. *The Sheffield Iris* commented that Parker and Shore's stoppage heralded the bleakest year for Sheffield and blamed the trade depression on the Corn Laws, which had a more ruinous influence on Sheffield than upon any other manufacturing district. Manufacturers had to obtain credit to export to America, because imports from there were not allowed.

101. The Hall of Science on Blackfriars Road; it was the headquarters of the National Union of Working Classes.

102. Introduction, note 18; he spoke for two hours and was listened to by 1,200-1,500 people (*The Times,* 19 Jan. 1843).

103. *The Times* reported on an extraordinary depression of the barometer on Friday, 13 Jan. 1843, the day before the hurricane. Damage was widespread, with eye-witness accounts mostly from coastal districts all over the country appearing in the paper. A national appeal for help for stricken areas was printed in *The Times* on 19 Jan. 1843.

104. The advertisement offered the services of a young person to teach children of 12 or 13 years of age in the usual studies, French and Latin grammar, and music to beginners. Mr Murphy was a wholesale confectioner. (*Morning Chronicle,* 19 Jan. 1846).

105. St George the Martyr, High Street, Southwark.

106. Adelaide Gallery, Lowther Arcade, West Strand; popular lectures and experiments were held there, as well as concerts in the Royal Adelaide Hall. (advertisements in *The Times; Tallis's London Street Views,* 1839).

107. Drummond died a few days later.

108. Surrey Chapel.

109. A district of Southwark round St George the Martyr's church.

110. Introduction, note 52; see also entry for 31 Jan.

111. Gerard's Hall, Basing Lane, (cf. T. Pennant, *Some Account of London,* (4th ed., 1805), p. 339.)

112. The first 'opium war' with China ended with the Treaty of Nanking and the cession of Hong Kong to Britain in August, 1842. The British attempt to annex Afghanistan can hardly be described overall as a victory; presumably the punitive expedition to Kabul in September, following the massacre of a British force in January, is being referred to.

113. Mary Jenkinson, born 1826, aged 17 in 1843.

114. John Platts, Joseph's brother-in-law, married Ann Jenkinson in 1835.

115. Introduction, note 47.

116. The Chartist meeting scheduled for September, 1843.

117. Introduction, note 48.

118. Introduction, p. 23.

119. Possibly Elizabeth, daughter of Rev. David Clark of Dronfield Independent church; she would be 23 in 1843; she died in November, 1853. Cf. Introduction, note 25.

120. Possibly Bowlers: see Appendix II.

Appendix I: Hatting Terms

B 1 and Bx: hat sizes.

Beaver: fur used for hats; cheeck or cheek beaver and white wooms beaver were the names given to fur of different qualities from different parts of the animal's body.

Blocking: the process of pulling the triangular hood over a wooden or metal hat block so as to give a hat shape with crown and brim. The hood was pulled down over the block with a tight string and the point of the hood flattened to make a crown.

Bodies: the body or shell of the hat before covering with the chosen material. Light body or stout were of different weights. A wool body was one made of wool to be covered with fur or woven silk.

Bowing: using the hatter's bow, a long wooden pole with bridges at each end between which catgut was stretched and which was suspended above the bowing workbench; with it the hatter caused vibrations in the downy mass of fur or wool fibres; these then settled into a layer which was covered with a damp cloth and the process repeated to form a second layer, the two layers being brought together into the large, loose conical hood.

Carrotting: fur was cut from the pelt or skin of an animal such as a rabbit or hare, the coarse hairs being pulled out by hand and discarded. The skins were then treated with a compound of mercury to make the fibres felt more easily, the process being called carroting because it turned the fur orange in colour. It could cause mercury poisoning, hence the saying 'as mad as a hatter'.

Clippings: probably bits of fur left over from shearing or other processes which could be used in hat mixtures.

D1, E1: hat sizes.

Fancies: a type of hat for children.

Felting: also called planking: the hoods were dipped in very hot acidulated water and rolled with a wooden pin, thus matting the fibres. Felting was carried out in a hat battery where six or eight planks were arranged in a circle, sloping inwards towards a central kettle or cauldron holding water heated from a fire below.

Finishing: process carried out by finishers who ironed the hats to shape, sheared the nap to the right length and curled the brim as necessary.

Hogsheads of plates: a plate was an inferior stuff hat, Spanish, Kent or Shropshire wool being used for the nap, or plate, instead of beaver's fur. They were presumably packed in casks.

Jerries: a cheap type of hat.

Low cro. hoods: a low crown type of hat; Bowlers, hat manufacturers, gave their name to the low crown Bowler hat.

Makers: body makers employed by a hatter.

Nappings: fur used for ruffing or putting a finer nap on a hat.

Nutria: the fur of the coypu, used as an alternative to beaver when that became expensive.

Planking: felting in hot acidulated water.

Plates: see under hogsheads. Thomas Jenkinson sent many dozens of 'planter's plates' to Jamaica between 1835 and 1838.

Pod: a measure by bulk.

Proofing: water-proofing to increase the water resistance of the hat.

Proofs: hats which had been proofed and blocked but not finished.

Odd fine bodies: fine hat bodies made up in quantities, not by dozens which was more usual.

Odd hats: hats not in dozens.

Red wool: part of the body of a beaver hat, from the llama or vicuna.

Rolled hats: a process in hatmaking, a form of ruffing.

Round, given out to: probably the giving out of hats to be ironed.

Ruffing: the felting of a fine cover on to a cheaper body, which was felted from wool, after which a layer of fur was felted on to the surface of the body to give a fine finish.

Rustics: a type of country hat.

Sax. wool: Saxony wool, a very fine quality.

Shells: hat bodies.

Silk hatting: a change in fashion in the 1840s made silk hats popular. Silk hats were made by pulling a woven silk plush cover over a body made of thin felt, or, more usually of stiffened gingham or other fabric. It was less skilled than felt hatting, which required a seven year apprenticeship.

Stout hat: a heavy, strong hat.

Stuff body: the body or shell of a stuff hat.

Stuff hat: hats made of rabbit, hare, nutria or beaver fur. The mixture varied according to the quality of the hat.

Stumped: One of the later stages in planking or felting.

Tare: allowance made for the weight of a container.

Tipping: the final finish of a hat before despatch to shop or customer. Tippers were usually women.

Trimmers: Usually women who inserted and stitched hat bands and linings.

Verdigris: a green dye.

Wet off: part of the proofing process.

White wooms: see beaver.

Wool hats: wool for these had to be carded before being made into the triangular hoods and planked, steeped, blocked and finished as for felt hats.

Dr. J.H. Smith supplied meanings for the majority of the hatting terms in this appendix; other information was taken from a letter to the *Morning Chronicle* by Henry Mayhew in 1850 and from G. Dobb's *A Day at a Hat-factory'* (1843). Stockport Museums and Art Gallery also helped by making their bibliographies and publications available.

Appendix II: Firms mentioned in the Diary

Those which also occur in Thomas Jenkinson's account book are marked *.

*Airds: Benjamin Lambert Aird, 1 Royal Street, Lambeth, draper; also at 6 Mount Street, Lambeth.

Bates: John Bates, skinner and furrier, Long Lane, Boro'.

*Booth: Henry Booth & Son were hat manufacturers, 26 Snig Hill, Sheffield. James Booth, hat manufacturer, Denton, Manchester. J. H. Booth, hatters, Pomona Street and Lord Street, Liverpool.

Borrodaile: Wm and Geo. Borrodaile, furriers and skinners, Southwark Bridge Road; also Borrodaile and Ismay of Bridge Road, Southwark.

Bowker: Possibly Bowler, John and Benjamin, hat makers, 59 Castle Street, Southwark; Bowler & Son also manufacturers on Blackfriars Road; the bowler hat was their creation.

*Cooper: E. Cooper, hat manufacturer, Castle Street, Southwark.

*Davenport & Sons: James Davenport, hat manufacturer, Knifesmithgate, Chesterfield. See also Stringfellow.

Dixon: see Whiting.

*Ellwoods: Ellwood & Sons, hat manufacturers, 24 Great Charlotte Street, Blackfriars. Also Wm Ellwood, hatter, Castle Street, Southwark.

Evans Bros: (*J. Evans of Bristol.) Evans Bros. were coopers and manufacturers of yeast in Southwark.

*Felix: Edward Felix, 10 Cheapside, hat manufacturer.

Fullers: John Fuller & Co., 96 Long Lane, Southwark, hat manufacturer.

*Hoyle: Edward Hoyle is described as being of Oldham, but later diary references are to Hoyle of Manchester and Hoyle & Newbury of Manchester, who were silk and smallware manufacturers making sewing silks, umbrellas, hat linings, trimmings and galloons.

*Ivyleafe: James Ivyleafe, hatter and manufacturer, 139 Regent Street.

Jarratt: George Jarratt, hatter, 199 Piccadilly; also a Jarratt at the Marquis of Granby public house, Union Street, Southwark, 1832-4.

*Leech and Robinson: Charles William Robinson and James William Leech, tailors, 42 High Street, Oxford. They split the partnership c.1842, each with premises on High Street.

*Lumsden & Co.: linen and woollen drapers and haberdashers, 33 Denny Street, Tralee, Co. Kerry.

*Moule: Isaac Moule, tailor, 70 Friar Street, Reading, 1837 and tailor and draper, 43 Minster Street, 1842.

*Payne Bros: possibly Payne & Flower, hat dyers, Tooley Street, Southwark or George Payne, hatter, 62 Long Lane, Bermondsey.

*Scott: Wm Scott, Wood Street, Wakefield, hair cutter, perfumer and hat dealer. (The account book also mentions supplying Scott with wigs.)

*Spencer: Thomas Henry Spencer, hatter, 4 Old Bond Street, Bath.

*Stringfellow: with Davenports, Stringfellows were manufacturing hatters on Burlington Street, Chesterfield.

*Tate: James Tate, hatter, 10 Lord Street, Liverpool.

*Walker & Gordon: James Walker and Thomas Gordon, linen drapers, Blackfriars.

Whitings & Dixon: James Burgess Whiting, hat manufacturer, 76 High Street, Southwark; A. Dixon, hat manufacturer, 156 Union Street, Southwark.

Directories consulted for information on firms: *Critchett's London Post Office Directory*, 1832; *Glover's Directory of Derbyshire*, 1829; *White's Directory of Derbyshire*, 1857; *Post Office Directory of London*, 1852; *Robson's London Directory*, 1832; *Post Office Directory of London*, 1846. Information was also supplied by libraries at Bath, Bristol, Manchester, Reading, Oxford, Wakefield and Tralee, co. Kerry, Ireland, whose help is gratefully acknowledged.

Appendix III: Dronfield people mentioned in the Diary

Allen, E.: Probably Edward Allen, a file cutter, on the electoral register for 1832, with a freehold house on Farwater Lane.

Booth, Wm.: One of seven names on the reconstituted church roll of Dronfield Independent Church when the Rev. David Clark took over in 1813; had previously offered his kitchen for the use of worshippers until the new chapel was completed in 1812.

Butterman, Wm: Besides being owner of Butterman's School in what became known as Machin's Yard, this man was also a coal owner and landowner.

Camm, Wm: Aged 18 in 1825 in the records of the Friendly Sick Club, he became part of the Ward, Camm and Siddall partnership making spindles at the Damstead Works; an associate of George Ward, Joseph Jenkinson's brother-in-law.

Cecil family: John Rotherham bought Dronfield manor in 1756; the heiress Elizabeth Rotherham died 1797 leaving it to Joseph Cecil, who died in 1827. It was his widow Jane Catherine Cecil to whom Joseph referred in 1833. The Rotherham-Cecils are still lords of Dronfield.

Clark, Rev. David: Minister to the Dronfield Independent Church; his first ministry was 1813-19 and his second 1829-43. He lived at Cliffe House and died in 1848.

Coope, Joseph: William Coope was innkeeper of the White Swan in the 1790s; he died a few years before Joseph started his diary. Joseph Coope was his son.

Dobb: Thomas Dobb first appears in Dronfield in the land tax assessment for 1818, paying for 'works'. The baptisms of six of his children is noted in the parish register, 1820-33, but not that of Forbes, who was presumably the eldest and born before the family came to Dronfield.

Earnshaw: Licensee of the Red Lion at the Corner of Church Street and Lea Road, now demolished.

Flint, M.: There was a family of this name at the Heart of Oak on Northern Common later in the century.

Fowler, J.: James Fowler was a cordwainer near the Blue Stoops in the census of 1851; the Fowlers were a prolific Dronfield family often mentioned as being letter receivers for the Post Office.

Gratton, James: a tailor in Stoops Yard, licensee of the Green Dragon and a member of the Peel Monument Committee (cf. p. 24).

Hollingworth: a shopkeeper.

Havenhand, Mark: an assistant overseer living on Church Street in 1851, the Havenhands being a numerous family in Dronfield, both then and later in the century.

Hydes: tenants of Manor Farm on High Street and also, at another time, of the farm at Hallowes.

Jackson, George: grocer in High Street.

Jenkinson, Ann: Joseph's sister, born 1814, married to John Platts.

Jenkinson, David: Joseph's younger brother, born 1815.

Jenkinson, Elizabeth: Joseph's mother.

Jenkinson, Elizabeth: Joseph's younger sister, born 1812, married George Ward of the Damstead Works 1833.

Jenkinson, Harriet: Joseph's younger sister, born 1824.

Jenkinson, James: Joseph's younger brother, born 1818.

Jenkinson, John: Joseph's youngest brother.

Jenkinson, Luke: Joseph's father, died 1848.

Jenkinson, Mary: Joseph's sister, born 1826.

Jenkinson, Thomas: Joseph's uncle, died 1843.

Jenkinson, Thomas: Joseph's cousin, born 1810.

Joell, E. and Joell, Mark: Mark Joell died in 1835; he was a member of the Independent Church. Joells are listed in directories as coopers.

Lee, Robert: a woodcutter, mentioned in the letter from the Dobb family in Philadelphia.

Lucas, Edward: The younger of the three brothers who came to Sheffield in 1787 from Birmingham where their father had been a silver refiner. He took over the Dronfield foundry in 1811 and lived in Vale House. He is said to have been present, at the age of 90, at the inauguration of the Peel Monument in 1854.

Lucas, Samuel: Probably the son of Edward, born 1800 and already in his father's firm by 1822 when Edward Lucas and Son appeared in the Sheffield section of Edward Baines' *Yorkshire Directory*.

Nicholson, John: a surgeon in Dronfield until the 1860s, there being a partnership between him and James Wright in 1835. Nicholson must have been a young man, perhaps just beginning his practice, when Joseph went to him with his influenza in 1833, since his age in 1851 was given as 45. He lived at Knott House, now the Royal Bank of Scotland.

Platts, John: a spindlemaker, married Joseph's sister Ann in 1833.

Schofield, William: a weaver in Dronfield, mentioned in R. E. Leader, *History of the Cutler's Company in Hallamshire*, vol. II (1905) when his sons were apprenticed in 1809 and 1813. A William Schofield is also listed as a linen draper in Pigot's *Commercial Directory*, 1828 and in Glover's *Derbyshire Directory*, 1829. He was a foundation member of Dronfield Independent Church in 1812-13 and died in 1835; he may have lived in what was Ward's Yard or Fanshaw Cottages on High Street.

Slack, William: Joseph Jenkinson refers to 'Aunt Slack', so William may have been a cousin; a John Slack kept the Blue Posts (Stoops) in 1809 and Peter Slack kept it in 1828-9.

Seston, George: a coalminer who seems to have lived in what have become known as Butler's Cottages on Lea Road.

Ward, George: Joseph's brother-in-law, husband of his sister Elizabeth, whom he married in 1833. Probably born c.1808, the son of Samuel Ward of Dore.

Ward, Robert: a manufacturer of sugar of lead (lead acetate) listed as a manufacturing chemist in directories 1828-57. The works was on the Frith Brook, the boundary between Dronfield and Unstone. He built Wreakes House on Wreakes Lane and had as his tenant in another house his partner and Joseph Jenkinson's friend, Thomas Dobb, before the Dobb family emigrated to Philadelphia in 1833. Henry Jenkinson, Ward's son-in-law, carried on the works until the building of the Wilson Cammell steel rail-making plant in 1872-3 obliterated the site.

Ward, Samuel: probably a shoemaker, living near Luke Jenkinson's house.

INDEX

Note: there may be more than one reference to a subject or person on the page indicated. Incidental references to place-names (e.g. streets etc. merely passed through during walking) are not indexed. A question mark before a page reference indicates uncertainty whether the person or firm concerned is actually meant.